DATE DUE

MAR 27 1995   FEB 2 8 1995

People and Policy
in the
Middle East

This book has been prepared under the auspices of
The Center for International Affairs, Harvard University

Created in 1958, the Center fosters advanced study of basic world problems by scholars from various disciplines and senior officers from many countries. The research at the Center, focusing on the processes of change, includes studies of military-political issues, the modernizing processes in developing countries, and the evolving position of Europe. The research programs are supervised by Professors Robert R. Bowie (Director of the Center), Alex Inkeles, Henry A. Kissinger, Edward S. Mason, Thomas C. Schelling, and Raymond Vernon.

A list of Center publications will be found at the end of this volume.

Max Weston Thornburg

People and Policy
in the
Middle East

A Study of Social and Political Change
as a Basis for United States Policy

W · W · NORTON & COMPANY · INC · *New York*

First Edition

Library of Congress Catalog Card No. 64-10575

Published simultaneously in the Dominion of
Canada by George J. McLeod Limited, Toronto

PRINTED IN THE UNITED STATES OF AMERICA
FOR THE PUBLISHERS BY THE VAIL-BALLOU PRESS, INC.

123456789

To all the helpful faculty,

research and staff members at

the Center for International Affairs

Contents

Introduction

by Edward S. Mason

MAX THORNBURG once acquired an island in the Persian Gulf, a strip of sand so barren that not one blade of vegetation existed on it. He drilled for water and reached it 350 feet down, and some years later the island was a little paradise, with trees and flowers in profusion, gardens, pools, lawns, and a handsome dwelling. The full story of that transformation is another book, which remains to be written by his devoted wife, Leila. The present volume, which Thornburg finished shortly before he died in September 1962, is not about change in physical surroundings but about change in people—a subject that fascinated him even more.

Thornburg was trained as an engineer and was graduated from the University of California in 1917. After serving three years in the U.S. Army and becoming a captain, he joined, in 1920, the staff of the Standard Oil Company of California. He was chief engineer of the manufacturing department of his company from 1924 to 1929, manager of the important Richmond Refinery, 1929 to 1931, and chairman of the board of engineers from 1931 to 1936. He was, thus, forty-four years old and an established figure in the West Coast petroleum industry when he was asked to go as an executive to supervise the newly established oil operations of his own and associated companies in the Persian Gulf.

Anyone who has lived and worked for any length of time in the less-developed countries of the Middle East, Africa, and Asia has experienced the frustration of discovering that practices, organizations, and techniques of proven value in Chicago, Manchester, or Essen work haltingly or not at all in Kampala, Shiraz, or Dacca. The imported machinery may be the same; the filing cabinets may look similar; but the response of people individually or in groups to ideas, suggestions, orders, and pleas may be decidedly different. For some Westerners the frustration is so overwhelming that return to the home environment at the earliest possible moment becomes imperative. Others become curious as to why some things won't work and set themselves to the study of modifications and adaptations that may, over a period of time, have some chance of making them work.

Thornburg was one of those who stayed, tried, experimented, and adapted and later came home to reflect on his years of experience in the Middle East as oil executive, engineer, consultant, and trusted adviser to governments. He was in a position to employ the best talent the West could provide in the shape of lawyers, engineers, agronomists, economists, and doctors, and he did so. But none of these specialists, he lamented, possessed an "organized source of guidance in the one field that produced most of our problems—the field of social behavior."

During the many years he spent in the Middle East, Thornburg was in an excellent position to observe social behavior in every sphere. The countries of the Middle East which had been static and somnolent for generations were beginning to respond to the winds of change. The heavy but palsied hand of Ottoman dominance had been removed. The First World War had seen the desert sands shifted and broken by the tread of Western armies. Tribal dynasties came to power in new countries. The radio and other means of mass communication brought a realization of a broader world. The rapid expansion of oil exploration and production was accompanied by a flood of technicians and bustling Western businessmen. These impulses and incentives to change impinged on highly traditionalist societies devoted to inherited ways.

Thornburg was deeply interested in how and why the people responded as they did to these outside influences. His period of residence in the Middle East began in 1936, when as Vice President of the Bahrain Petroleum Company and of the California-Texas Oil Company he moved to Bahrain Island in the Persian Gulf. This little shaikhdom under the governance of its hereditary rulers, the Al Khalifah family, advised and influenced by an extraordinary representative of Britain, Charles Belgrave, was already responding to Western influences. The development of its oil resources and the inflow of Western technicians and money led to the employment of thousands of Arabs in activities as far removed from their traditional pearl diving, fishing, and goat herding as can be imagined. Here, working closely with the people as well as with their leaders, Thornburg was in the center of the dramatic clash between East and West, old and new. Here, too, the patriarchal ruler of Bahrain gave him the tiny nearby island of Umm A'Sabaan where he and his wife made their Persian Gulf home. The activities of housebuilding, gardening, sailing, and fishing gave them further intimate opportunities to observe when and how changes in technique can be introduced into a traditionalist environment.

With the coming of World War II, Thornburg was called to Washington, where he served three years in the important position of Petroleum Adviser to the Department of State. It was during this period that I first became acquainted with him; I admired his enormous capacity for dividing scarce supplies among demanding claimants with a minimum of friction and a maximum of tact. After the war, while maintaining his home in the Persian Gulf, he undertook a number of consulting assignments. In 1947 he directed an Economic Survey of Turkey. From 1948 to 1951, as chairman of a group of advisers from Overseas Consultants, Inc., he helped prepare Iran's first Seven-Year Plan. He returned to Turkey in 1954–1955 to assist in preparing an industrial plan for the government of that country. From this and his previous experience, he co-authored a study called *Turkey: An Economic Appraisal.**

After some twenty years of experience in and close observation of the Middle East, Thornburg was appointed Regents Professor of Political Science at the University of California and was asked to reflect on this experience and to convey its meaning to colleagues and students. This assignment was followed by three years at the Center for International Affairs at Harvard, which he devoted to consultation with social scientists and the preparation of the manuscript for this volume.

In his book, Thornburg has carefully evaluated his years of personal experience in the Middle East. It is his belief that the practical men in the field—men who represent the political and economic interests of the Western democracies—and the social theorists, who have perhaps studied the area from a more detached and impersonal point of view, should work more closely together in understanding and influencing change in the Middle East. The practitioners and the policymakers, in his words, need a "framework of concepts within which reason has established a certain order—to guide judgment as to what is significant and what is not." The key to understanding the Middle East, he feels, is in understanding the people themselves. His book is an inquiry into the be-

---

* Max Weston Thornburg, Graham Spry, and George Soule, *Turkey: An Economic Appraisal.* New York: Twentieth Century Fund, 1949.

havior of people in the process of change, and an investigation of the nature of change itself as it has occurred in this area. He seeks the traditionalist springs of behavior in a study of the extended family system, the tribe, the village community and in the pervasive influence of Islam. He investigates sources and patterns of change as he has observed them; and he describes areas in which further observation and investigation is needed. His book, with its consistent emphasis on actual events, is both a warning and a plea to all of us to "look before we leap" into the Middle East or any of the lesser developed areas of the world.

Thornburg was a most interesting, stimulating, and provocative colleague. He was an unusual addition to an academic environment; a type that professors would like to get their hands on but usually do not succeed in so doing; a distinguished man of practical experience willing to share that experience and acquire more. In his association with his academic colleagues, and in his book, he has shed new light on the complex relationship between analysis and application, between the general and the concrete, between the word and the deed.

Preface

AFTER MORE than forty years of active professional life as an engineer, business executive, and consultant—the last half of it in "backward" countries—I had to explain to myself why I so often failed to do what I set out to do. No one expects an unbroken record of successes. But we Americans have set one high standard of accomplishment; no job can be considered done unless it works. What bothered me was that the second half of my professional life, spent largely in Turkey, Persia, and the Arab countries, seemed to demonstrate that I didn't know how to do the things that the first half had proved I could do. I did what I had learned to do, but the results were not what I expected. Jobs which I thought had been done didn't work; or after a brief period stopped working. This, moreover, seemed to apply equally to other Americans, in both private and government undertakings.

One generalization seemed clear. The greater the extent to which the *people* of an underdeveloped society took part in a given project, the less predictable the outcome. And when the part they took included important decision-making, predictability vanished almost completely. Clearly, people were part of the problem; but what is there to be known about people, except the kinds of things that we learn by living and working with them?

To this last question the social scientists answered, "Plenty!" I had an opportunity to find out what they meant in 1954 when I occupied the post of Regents Professor at the University of California—an honorary lectureship that enabled me to share my problems with Peter Odegard, Thomas Blaisdell, George Lenczowsky, Rupert Emerson (visiting that year from Harvard), and other scholars. But on the whole it seemed to me that social scientists were concerned with people in the abstract. Their people were referred to as *ego* and *alter*, were parts of social systems, had institutions, responded to mores, or were mere victims of historical accidents. My people were real persons—Mehmet, Hassan, and Abdullah—who lived in villages or cities or roamed the desert. My people had the same vices and virtues that we have, but exhibited them in different ways, often when least expected.

During the next three years—increasingly troublous ones in the Middle East—I spent what time I could in New York working on my own limited aspects of the broader problems then under study by panels of specialists organized by the Rockefeller Brothers Fund. It was during this period that I began to synthesize what seemed to be the essentials of my problem—which, as I saw it then, was to find out what produced change in a traditional society and how that change could be guided.

In 1958 I was invited to pursue that inquiry at Harvard University at the Center for International Affairs (jointly, for two years, with the Center for Middle Eastern Studies). Here, if anywhere, I should have been able to find the help and direction that I needed. I learned much that I had not known about what goes on in a modern university. I had come to believe, with many others, that most research aimed at broadening and deepening our understanding of the world dealt with the physical or natural sciences, which to me were not a bit more "natural" than the behavior of a tribe. Perhaps the most important thing I learned was that serious research scholars in the various fields of social science were as interested in my observations and perplexities concerning behavior in traditional societies, and in the impact of our ways upon them, as I was in learning what discoveries had been made and what theories evolved to explain their behavior. I found no "ivory tower." Give or take a few premises as to relative importance, our interests were much the same.

I did find wide gaps to be bridged between us. Bridges must be built from both ends, but first we must know where to build them. A conventional first step is to make a reconnaissance sketch of the region, showing the areas that are to be linked together, and the various passes and chasms between. With this as a basis a few traverses can be run to determine the selection of a route. This book is my own reconnaissance in a region that is important to all of us. I have approached it as a practitioner in policy-making and implementation. My traverses have been run from that side. The areas to be linked together are the Middle East and the West, and the seemingly separate fields of the policy-maker and the social scientist. The traffic to be moved is ideas, understanding, principles, methods, and means. I have not been able to complete this bridge, but I hope I have been able to show where it should be built.

People and Policy

in the

Middle East

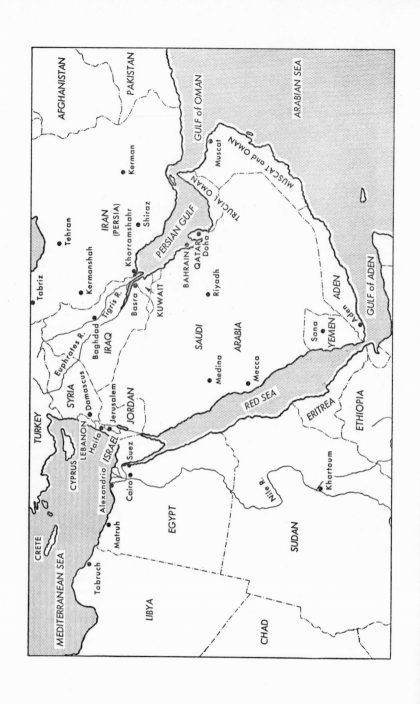

Chapter One

Wanted: A Basis for Policy

THE THINGS WE Americans have done in the underdeveloped countries have not furthered either their interests or ours as much as we expected. There is also evidence to show that what the peoples of those countries have done has not met their own expectations, and that there is an increasing tendency among them to lay some part of the blame at the door of the West. To say this is not to depreciate either our intentions or our performance. We can take just pride in most aspects of both. But despite the record of accomplishments it seems clear that expectations in the "traditional" societies have outrun achievements. The complexity of the problems that confront us has risen faster than our demonstrated capacity to meet them.

Either expectations must be modified or accomplishments must be increased—perhaps both. Otherwise a sense of frustration may overtake us, or those countries themselves, and result in a decision to abandon courses which in the main have been in the right direction.

Until a few years ago, about the end of the war, Americans were trusted because we had no political or "imperialistic" aspirations, and were respected because we had become the most powerful nation on earth. Both of these things can still be said about us; nevertheless, the respect and prestige that we used to enjoy have declined at an alarming rate. This has happened despite the fact that what we regard as mutual strategic and economic interests have increased greatly during the same period, as have also the programs of military, economic, and technical aid that were intended to serve these mutual interests.

Questions arise. Has it been our own conduct in the less-developed countries that has raised doubts concerning our aims and the efficacy of our means? If so, why have our efforts to improve the conditions and win the confidence of those peoples fallen short of their purpose? These questions raise a more pressing one: whatever the reasons, what can we do now to reverse these unfavorable trends?

To examine these questions over the full range of American interests in all the newly developing countries of the world would introduce so many variables—economic, cultural, historical, and social—that the problem of identifying and interrelating fundamentally significant factors might be unmanageable. On the other hand, too narrow a focus upon particular situations might tend to exaggerate the significance of accidental factors, and fail to disclose generalizations that indicate order in the developmental process. A middle course is possible. Most of the underdeveloped countries fall naturally into a few main groups, delimited generally by geographic, ethnic, cultural, linguistic, and economic boundaries within which at least these variables are reduced to a manageable range. This makes it possible, within such an area, to identify other variables more readily. Generalizations reached on this basis may then have broader application, since the main characteristics of "traditional" societies are common to most newly developing countries.

The Middle East is one such group. Broad generalizations apply to it as a whole, but within it there are differences that cover nearly the full range from "traditional" to "modern" societies. What answers can be found to the questions just raised, as they apply to the Middle East? What lessons can be learned?

American entry into Middle East affairs was mainly through private, not government, activities. First there were the schools and hospitals founded by our missionaries beginning more than one hundred years ago, which will be an everlasting credit to the American name. More recently American oil companies brought prosperity and other innovations to limited groups. Other private institutions have played important parts. But in the days following the First World War—fateful ones for the Middle East—the British and French parceled the spoils between themselves, through the mandates that they contrived without much thought for the people of the Middle East. While this went on, our own government looked the other way. Even as late as 1940, after the outbreak of the Second World War, our lack of official concern was illustrated by a brief note that President Roosevelt wrote with his own hand to dispose of a perplexing file submitted to him by an aide: "Arabia is too far afield for us. Can't you get the British to do something?" *

Since that note was written it has become increasingly clear that neither Arabia nor its neighbors are as far afield

---

* The file, submitted to the President by Harry Hopkins, set out the dilemma of the Arabian American Oil Company which, to safeguard its concession, had acceded to demands of King Ibn Saud for cash advances then totaling approximately seven million dollars. At that time the attitude of the King toward the Allies and Germany was uncertain. Since part of the cash was used for the purchase of military arms, the oil company demurred at accepting responsibility for further financing in advance of earned royalties and referred the matter to the Department of State with the consequences noted. I was permitted to see the file after it had been returned to the State Department bearing the President's notation.

as we used to think. The changes that have brought them within the perimeter of our anxious attention have been developments that in many instances threatened both our national security and our economic interests, two dominant concerns of our foreign policy.

Americans have had a hand in bringing about some of these developments. There was our part in the partition of Palestine. We have had several military programs in the Middle East, including our unsuccessful effort to create a Middle East defense pact. We promoted the "northern tier" concept, ending, without us, in the Baghdad Pact. We established air bases or military airfields in Libya and Saudi Arabia. We took a leading part in restoring Persia's oil industry following the Mossadegh nationalization—after our earlier indifference toward the events that led to that affair. We gave moral support to Egypt's demand that the British evacuate that country. We conducted a widespread but somewhat erratic program of economic and technical aid. These and other manifestations of our growing interest at the government level reached a peak when we frustrated British and French efforts to resolve by force the Suez Canal nationalization problem, maintained a neutral posture in respect to the French difficulties in North Africa, proclaimed the Eisenhower Doctrine, and resorted to a show of our own armed strength by parading our sea and air forces when trouble threatened in Syria, and by landing our marines in Lebanon.

These and other actions that our government has taken—I do not refer to them collectively as a "policy"—have established us as a factor to be reckoned with, but have not established any basis for the reckoning. Their result on the whole probably has been less to determine the outcome of fundamental issues than to intensify pressures in particular situations, in some cases raising them to a level of danger that might not otherwise have been reached.

If it is accepted that our government's activities in the Middle East have played only a secondary role in determining the broad trend in affairs there, where can we look for the underlying forces that during the past few decades have activated and given direction to the events that we are witnessing today? To those of us who have lived in the region and watched it change over a period of years, it seems clear that the fundamental causes of the perplexing behavior and apparent animosities that face us must be sought in the changes that have been brought about by and within the Middle East peoples themselves.

Until comparatively recently, most of the changes that have been taking place there over the last twenty-five or thirty years have been of a kind that seemed commendable to one brought up in the American tradition. The overthrow of tyrannical despotisms in Turkey and Persia and of a dissolute monarchy in Egypt were in keeping with our precepts of democracy. The welding together of tribal communities into a strong Arab Kingdom under Ibn Saud formed a union that brought strength to all its parts. The preparations, under some form of British tutelage, for independent government in other Arab states, parallel American policy in the Philippines. The development of latent economic resources is typical of the American way, as is also the spread of new ideas through new channels of social communication. Above all, the awakening of millions of starved, diseased, illiterate, politically and socially oppressed peoples to the belief that they don't have to go on in this way finds a sympathetic and understanding response in American hearts. Collectively, these changes have signaled the revolution through which a new Middle East will in time emerge from the old.

Superimposed upon these internal changes have been the increasing interests of foreign powers in the area. In modern times these were mainly British, Russian, and French. Recently we have entered the picture. Even more recently the Soviet Union has acted vigorously not only to carry forward the age-old expansionist program of the Czars, but to win the entire area over to the Communist ideology. For this purpose the Communists have used the same tools of economic and technical aid that we had regarded as exclusively ours, plus other techniques that we have not yet learned—or at least have not chosen to employ for our own purposes.

It is against this metamorphosis of the Middle East over the past generation, and particularly its swiftly moving present currents, that we must examine our position and determine our policy.

American policy, as the term is commonly understood, is not confined solely to policies formulated and implemented by the Department of State, or by other official agencies of the government. It includes the decisions that are made by many other persons and institutions—also the reasons for which they are made. Decisions made and actions taken by the board of directors of a private corporation with international operations may have an impact upon American relations with another country more significant than many statements issued officially or communicated through formal diplomatic channels. Also writers, commentators, educators, and others who mold public opinion at home and express American viewpoints abroad, take part in formulating American policy. And in the United States, private citizens play some part in expressing the opinions and establishing the principles upon which official American policy is based.

The need exists today as never before for clear American policies in the Middle East. There are many reasons. We have important economic and strategic interests there. The British influence, upon which we depended for many years as a stabilizing factor, no longer exists as such. The current epidemic of government coups faces us with rapidly changing political structures. The intensification of Communist penetration makes the Middle East one of the principal fronts in our contest with Communist powers.

But there is another reason. Those countries, generally speaking, have entered a period and process of revolution, corresponding to although not directly comparable with the social, political, and economic revolutions through which the Western countries passed from the fourteenth to the nineteenth centuries. At various rates they are passing, or will pass, from the early stage of rebellion to the later stage of advancement. Characteristically, rebellion is *against* something; the creative, forward-looking forces of revolution appear later. Toward what aims those forces will be directed remains to be disclosed.

In this same period, too, the United States has outgrown its role as a youth among nations, and is faced with worldwide responsibilities as a leading power. How it will appraise and discharge those responsibilities also remains to be seen.

Today both these quests for a definition of purpose—our own and that of the Middle East peoples—are meeting in the Middle East. American interests there compel our attention to that area. Their own need for a pattern to follow makes the Middle East countries attentive to the one we set. This is what Secretary Dulles referred to as "the force of the enlightened conduct and example of the United States." But in the Middle East, merely to refer to it is not enough.

What are the factors that should guide American policy, in both its formulation and its execution? The problem is stated in these limited terms, rather than asking, "What should our policy be?" The emphasis properly belongs on the factors to be considered. Our policy itself will have many facets, because of the many countries concerned, and will move with the times. Its principles and purposes will change only slowly; nevertheless it must be dynamic, keeping pace

with changing events. We must view our problem in both contexts. What are the factors that determine our principles
and purposes? What are the factors that determine our program of action?

Answers to these questions, of course, do not depend entirely upon our own decisions. The problem presents its most
difficult aspects when it enters the area of decision by others.
What makes the Middle East peoples decide to do what they
do? On the strength of my own observations I can say that
the main reason for the failure of Western techniques to
achieve the desired results has been that those applying the
techniques have not understood what the *reaction of the society* would be. This has been true whether the techniques
were applied by us or by others, and regardless of the technical skill demonstrated. The core of the problem lies in the
way all relevant factors interact to influence behavior and
produce the changes that constitute the process of growth in
those countries.

To identify these factors is pre-eminently the task of the
policy-maker. He appears in many guises. Some of them, on
the American side, have already been mentioned—government officials, businessmen, educators, journalists. But there
are policy-makers among the Middle East peoples too, and
among other peoples with interests in the Middle East. Essentially the policy-maker is a practitioner, not a theorist. He
is concerned with decisions that are followed by action, and
typically these actions produce change. The reasons for seeking one change rather than another will depend upon the
aims of the policy-maker. The possible range of such aims is
unlimited. Viewpoints may be different; decisions may conflict—although Middle East aims and American aims, in the
long view, appear to be generally compatible. In any case, the
problem focuses upon the ways in which change takes place
in a given country, and how one change rather than another

can be brought about. This provides a point of departure common to all policy-makers.

As I am a practitioner rather than a theorist, my approach is essentially empirical, and the relationships and interactions among behavioral factors first became evident to me mainly from what I observed. But observation is not enough. Policy-making needs more than that. Such order as exists in the complex behavior of mankind is more likely to be found in fundamentals than in evidence that is perceived directly. What is significant must be sought through reason, as well as with the eyes and the notebook. Theory, that is to say, is essential to understanding reality. The greater the number of factors that can be made common to both the theory and the reality, the better the explanation of the reality, and the further the extension of the theory.

Many policy-makers, even some in high positions, take too little guidance from theory. The very word is scorned by many operators in government or business. But if the policy-maker puts his faith solely in observation and "common sense" he will be deficient in criteria by which to judge the significance of what he observes, and to evaluate his own aims and the effects of his actions upon human behavior.

Of course, neither the empirical nor the theoretical approach alone will give the answers to policy problems. Together, they will at least give the best answers that can be reached. With the world as it is today, less than this is not enough.

The theorist has his function to perform in this process. The policy-makers have theirs at various levels of influence and responsibility. But every American must know more than has been common in the past about what to expect from the theorist and what to demand from the policy-maker for the more intelligent exercise of his responsibilities.

Chapter Two

The People and Their Ways

THE POLICY-MAKER stands in the operational area that concerns him and looks out over the scene. He sees evidence of many trends, some of which he might wish could be changed. But between the immediate effects that he knows how to produce and the behavior that he might wish could be changed lie the obscurities of an ancient culture in which the causes of that behavior are concealed. The changes that matter are in the way people live, work, think, and hope. Change starts from what already exists. This is where the policy-maker must begin.

If he is coming into the Middle East for the first time, he will approach it with certain preconceptions. He will find much that he expects, both in the traditional ways of a medieval society and in the startling evidences of modernity. As he stays on, living among the people and seeking to understand their ways, his first impressions will be adjusted by the differentiations he makes within generalities, and between groups that have advanced at different rates and from different starting points.

From my own experience I know that these adjustments are never-ending. What was strange becomes familiar, but that does not mean that it is understood. A random set of observations does not lead to a critical description of a society, a culture, or an economy. What is significant in human behavior is not so easily discovered.

What is the picture of the Middle East people and their ways that unfolds to the visiting Westerner? For one thing, it will be a disordered picture, confused by contradictions. Some things that at first seem trivial will be found later to illuminate other things that are not.

Geographically, the Middle East includes Turkey and Persia on the north, Egypt on the south, and the region between. Politically, it includes ten nations with membership in the United Nations (Turkey, Persia,* Iraq, Syria, Jordan, Lebanon, Saudi Arabia, Egypt, Yemen, and Israel); also the British Crown Colony of Aden, and a series of semi-independent (British-protected) Arab States lying along the easterly and southerly coasts of the Arabian Peninsula.† Except as special reference is made to them, Israel and Aden are excluded from consideration here, as they are not subject to most of the generalizations that apply to the Middle East.

Racially, the population stock of the Middle East is quite diverse, but culturally there are enough broadly common characteristics to permit helpful generalizations when com-

---

* In most cases I use the name "Persia" rather than "Iran." The present Shah has said in his autobiography: "Recently, in response to a petition from a group of our statesmen and scholars, I have approved the use of both names interchangeably for all purposes." His Imperial Majesty Mohammed Reza Shah Pahlavi, *Mission for My Country*. New York: McGraw-Hill, 1961, p. 43.
† The British *Statesman's Year-Book* (London: Macmillan & Co., Ltd.) for 1960 lists ten Persian Gulf States (including Kuwait, which became independent in 1961), and refers to twenty-four principalities and shaikhdoms—some vaguely identified—in the Eastern and Western Aden Protectorates. Here I include the Sultanate of Muscat and Oman with the others, bringing the total to thirty-five.

paring the behavior of one group with that of another, or comparing different degrees of advancement. At least from the Byzantine period onward, and even earlier, great leveling forces have been at work to develop common attributes among these peoples, despite the counterinfluences affecting them variously from both internal and external sources. Islam gave them a common religion and a common code of daily life. Arabic, common to many of them as a daily language, and to all as the language of the Koran, brought their thinking toward a common pattern. Vast stretches of desert and unfertile mountains, interspersed with areas favorable for agriculture, imposed a general division into nomadic and settled ways of life, but at a level of bare subsistence for the majority. The once great Ottoman Empire included most of them for generations prior to the First World War, and did nothing to change the traditional social organization under which the mass of the people fought and raided under petty chiefs, or served as soldiers or slaves for the Kings and Caliphs. And more recently all alike have felt what it means to live at the much-talked-of "crossroads," where world powers contest for strategic and economic advantages.

But this is a highly generalized picture. What the newcomer meets first are individual persons. Here again there will be few early surprises. In his own country he has already met many people from these places, and found them little different from himself. If he is a member of a visiting mission, private or government, the people he first meets in Cairo, Istanbul, Beirut, Baghdad, or other principal cities, are likely to converse with him in good English or French, and to display the same sophistication that would be expected in, say, a corresponding group in Rome, Paris, or London. They talk about their own country and its problems with candor, and deprecate the ill-fortune that has overtaken it as a result of war, foreign exploitation, corruption in government, and deficiency of American aid.

Such a group might include government officials, leading businessmen, bankers, wealthy landowners, manufacturers, educators, and newspaper editors. Variously, from their different points of view, they will confirm and elaborate upon what is already quite generally known about their countries, and upon steps that have been or are about to be taken to put things right—insofar as this is possible with limited capital, and in the face of unenlightened or corrupt political machinations which admittedly exist. Foreign strategic, economic, and political interests, they will explain, have also intruded to complicate their problems. Frequently such discussions are held jointly with members of the American Embassy, and the tone of the assembly discloses no social or intellectual distinctions within it. Privately, the Embassy representatives may express misgivings as to the depth of the concern shown by this elite group in the basic problems of the country, and in that group's intentions to do more than deplore them.

During the last ten years or so another type has made an appearance; namely, the eager reformer, who seems to symbolize a new spirit in the Middle East. Socially, he may be a member of the old elite, or he may be the forerunner of a newly emerging middle class. He may be a politician, educator, editor, or businessman, but essentially he is a modernizer. His conversation marks him as being one step in advance of the others, in that he is concerned with *means* as well as with *ends,* and his mind bulges with Five- or Seven-Year Plans for the accelerated infusion of Western ideas, techniques, and capital. Because the means such reformers envisage are as Western as the ends toward which they are to be applied, the visiting Westerner sees a familiar and promising pattern of development, sponsored by a group possessing rather superior social and intellectual attainments. They speak our language along with several others, and, if one allows for understandable differences in experience and national viewpoints, seemingly think the way we do, and believe in what we believe in.

This first round of acquaintances, despite the warnings from our Embassy—and even their own warnings concerning each other—leaves Americans with the comforting impression that at least in discussions on economic theory, educational methods, investment and management problems, international questions, and art and culture, our experts and theirs stand on fairly common ground.

As the visitor moves away from these relatively Europeanized capital cities into the hinterland, he will be met by well-mannered young men in either European or picturesque native costumes, who, in quite good English, act as interpreters for their elders. In the Arab countries these elders are, on the whole, aristocrats in the Arab tradition, dignified, free from ostentation, wise in the lore of their people, reserved in their expression of opinion, and gracious in every way to their guests. Quite evident also is the deference in which they are held by their people. Here the Westerner's impression coincides with the conventional image of the Arab shaikh, modified perhaps by the realization that Western influences have already made a deep mark on the younger generation. This realization may suggest that advancement can be rapid, as tradition combines with modern ideas and techniques.

Everywhere he goes on this first round the visitor will be shown new works in progress—factories, power plants, irrigation systems, schools, hospitals, and government buildings, all of which had a place in his image because he knew these things were being done. At the same time, he cannot help seeing the widespread poverty and misery around him, which he also knew was there, but was not quite prepared to find in reality or to reconcile with his own sense of social justice.

On a visit to one of these capital cities I was once taken by a progressive-minded government Minister on a tour of new factories, and older ones with plans for extension. These were modern plants, capital-intensive and largely automatic, hence with little demand for labor. They were producing goods both for export and to replace imports, thus contributing to an improved foreign-exchange position as well as to an increased national income per capita. On our way back to his luxurious home, where I was a guest for the day, we passed a series of fields across each of which was strung a line of men, women, and children swinging their cumbersome hoes in the traditional way of tilling the soil. I interrupted the Minister's enthusiastic exposition of the industrial development program by pointing to these toiling peasants and asking where they fitted into his scheme. I had a feeling that he saw them for the first time, as anything but a familiar part of the landscape. He answered vaguely, "Oh, as the economy improves their lot will improve too, but meanwhile they are by no means as badly off as you Americans seem to think!" I could not say that he was wrong on either point, but as I reflected that they represented at least three-quarters of the rapidly expanding population, neither could I see how he was right.

Against this general background, conversations with acquaintances in these countries are illuminating. One thing is clear. Almost universally you will find that no one has faith in his government, as an institution. And often this also applies to nonpolitical institutions. Loyalty to individual leaders rather than to institutions is the rule. With the possible exception of Turkey, where government institutions came slowly to mean something apart from the individuals concerned, it is the man who is supported, sometimes quite blindly—not his government, his party or his program. Thus in Persia political "parties" exist only in a most elementary form, referred to locally as "fractions," which are nothing more than the followers of a particular leader within the parliamentary *majlis,* and which dissolve if that leadership ceases. It is only in the more politically mature countries that a party owes its identity to its principles or its goals, and survives continuing changes in leadership. To the visiting observer one of the most puzzling aspects of the Middle East political scene is this question of political parties—their origin and how they develop, what they stand for, and their function in the political process.

Another puzzling observation is that, although it is the man and not the institution who commands confidence and support, it is most often the impersonal concept or institution that becomes the object of hostility. Early American negotiators for oil concessions in the Arab countries learned quickly that it was always a few individuals who won the confidence and support of the Arabs, but it was always the *sharika* (company) that demonstrations and strikes were directed against. When anti-British and anti-Company hostility was at its height in Persia, at the time of Mossadegh's nationalization of the oil industry, the actual departure of the Company's head men was regretted as a personal loss by most who had known them. There is little doubt that it was anti-British—not anti-Glubb—hostility that was expressed in Jordan when Glubb Pasha was forced to leave. And again in Bahrain, when pressure was brought upon Sir Charles Belgrave to resign as Adviser to the Ruler, this was incidental to the current wave of hostility toward both the local government and the British, not a verdict against the man whom many thousands had come to regard as their personal benefactor. At this time the ruler of Bahrain himself was shown customary deference as he passed through rioting crowds, even while they shouted against his government. Throughout the Middle East, hostile attitudes are almost invariably directed against an impersonal concept or institution—capitalism, imperialism, colonialism; the British, French, or Americans; Israel or the foreign oil industry; NATO or the Baghdad Pact—or even their own government. Positive action, on the other hand, seems to require that the goal be personified in a man; even such nominally ideological movements as "Arab nationalism," "State nationalism," "Pan-Islamism," as well as various religious sects within Islam, appear to be associated primarily with a leader, more than with a principle.

As the visitor stays on in the Middle East, doing business in the several capital cities and making friends in both government and business circles, some of these early impressions begin to change. From his friends in government, whether ministers or senior civil servants, he learns that what was at first described to him as dark adumbrations of skulduggery within the government are in fact devices openly practiced and long condoned, if not exactly time-honored, for using public office for private ends. There is the simple diversion of government funds straight into private pockets without intermediate machinations. There are also complex collective operations through which one person after another takes an appropriate share for his part in enabling taxes to be evaded, profitable contracts awarded, purchasing agreements closed, foreign-exchange licenses obtained, import duties escaped, court action suspended, deputies elected, remunerative appointments made, roads built to private properties, and every other form of corruption and chicanery that we Americans have ever heard of in our worst municipal governments at home. The conclusion the observer is likely to reach is that, whereas such practices are exceptional at home and have little effect on the economy at large, they are wholesale in the Middle East, and have a paralyzing effect on the economy, partly because they are carried out on such a large scale in relation to the total economy, but even more because of the widespread mistrust they engender, creating an atmosphere of suspicion in which no man will trust another, and least of all the impersonal functional institutions of his government.

A commonly heard explanation for corruption in the lower ranks of government is that the salaries paid are so low that employees are compelled to filch from the funds that pass through their hands in order to meet the necessities of life. On the other hand, low salary scales have been candidly defended on the ground that they represent only part of what the employee makes from his job. In other cases, usually at higher levels, it appears to be generally accepted, although not regularized by law, that some reasonable share of monies collected is a perquisite of the office, and unless the incumbent becomes too greedy, no questions will be asked. The story is told of Ibn Saud that when a well-meaning friend urged him to get rid of his Finance Minister, who was said to be robbing him blind, the King answered, "What! Provide another fortune for a new man? No! He must have almost as much as he wants by now. Let him stay!" I do not vouch for the story, but it has the perfume of truth.

Widespread bribery and simple theft are bad enough, but more damaging are the practices that undermine the very foundations upon which a modern economy rests—respect for the law, justice in the courts, performance of contract, faithful trusteeship over funds invested by others, and a basic belief in fair dealing where no explicit rules apply. It can be said that in none of these countries are the interests of minority stockholders in private corporations effectively protected against virtual confiscation by the controlling interest. This is perhaps explanation enough for the prevailing reluctance to participate in share-capital undertakings (except in the traditional "family company"), a reluctance that shuts off the most important single method of capital formation that has been developed in the West. Many young men in these

countries have been trained in Europe as chartered accountants, the equivalent of certified public accountants in the
United States. But unless engaged in falsifying books with a
skill that evades detection, they would starve to death at their
trade. Public or legal audits are not the rule.

One time I was called upon to assist in the reorganization
of a group of government-owned textile factories through the
creation of a single corporation under the commercial code
of one of the Middle East countries. This, presumably, would
remove the textile factories from the reach of avaricious
politicians. The new board of directors included some of the
most prominent members of the community. Within a year
it was clear that the enterprise was bankrupt, despite an almost monopoly market and a demand that exceeded production. By published accounts this could be explained only as
an act of God. But an outraged group of young chartered
accountants came up with another explanation. The directors
of the government-owned corporation had created two new
companies owned by themselves. One bought up field cotton
at a rock-bottom price fixed by the government cotton-grader,
and then sold it to the corporation at a second price based
upon re-grading it as prime cotton. The government corporation then sold its finished product to the other private company at little more than cost, and the private company resold
it at the going market price. The accountants revolted because, as they explained, under rules that allowed such practices there was no professional career in sight for them. Although this particular operation was stopped, no indictments
followed, nor, apparently, was any prestige lost.

On another occasion I was spending the evening with a
Middle East friend who had been very helpful in getting a
social reform bill enacted, although this was outside his
ordinary duties in the government. I mention this only as an
indication of his public-mindedness. His secretary came in

and placed a small packet of papers on the table and departed without a word. My friend flicked them through with his thumb and turning to me said nonchalantly, "Paychecks. My phantom payroll." I was too familiar with this practice to need further explanation. He and many others could hire and fire fictitious government employees according to their need for funds, cashing the paychecks themselves.

During the last few years, under the urge for industrialization, many new private enterprises have been started in these countries, making use of credit and other aids provided by the government or available only with government approval. In these circumstances it is not surprising to find that officials having authority to grant or without that approval— or members of their families—turn up as substantial shareholders, even in businesses quite foreign to their customary interests. It would not be fair to say that in no case were these holdings actually paid for; government officials have the same right as others to invest their personal funds. But in one case with which I am familiar there was audible grumbling over the Prime Minister's claim—as reported— to first choice of these "courtesy" participations. And by other reports, which I have no way of verifying but do not dismiss as fantastic, even prime ministers must sometimes content themselves with second choice.

In reviewing this scene of tangled principles, the relatively small but growing group of sincere reformers must not be overlooked, including many men who seek public office because they are dedicated to the welfare of their country. All Westerners who have worked in these countries can name men of this type. Many of them work quietly, doing what they can to raise standards without breaking with the organization they are intent upon improving. Others are openly rebellious, alternating between government office and private status according to their political support of the moment. It is common to discover that leading businessmen have held high public offices in the past, but have left the government because they could no longer put up with its ways. Frequently, too, those classed as intellectuals and inducted into government service have left for the same reason, and now as teachers or writers support the reforms they know to be needed. At a growing rate such men as these are establishing new standards of conduct in both government and business, and giving substance to the vague ideals of the universally rebellious younger generation, who have no wish to follow in the steps of the older.

A few years ago my wife and I were visiting friends in the important textile manufacturing city of Adana, in southern Turkey. During the night a fire broke out in one of the mills and totally destroyed it. The following morning we visited the scene, where firemen were still fighting the flames in baled cotton stored in one end of the plant. With our friend we worked our way through the crowd to the other end, where we were introduced to the owner. He was directing the work of a wrecking crew dismantling the smoldering remains of the building. He took time to point to some dump trucks and a steam shovel just pulling up to the site, and said, "Within an hour we'll have new foundations started for a bigger and better plant!" A question from our friend brought the answer. News of the fire had been flashed during the night to Istanbul, and had been heard by the head of a private Turkish insurance company, a former minister who had left the government to build his own business on his own business standards. He had at once telephoned the mill-owner, whose insurance he carried, and told him that his loss would be covered in full and to lose no time in rebuilding. In the West this might not be surprising, but in Turkey it shows a new spirit at work. To create a private insurance company with local capital and build it into a nationwide institution is not easy, and is possible only if a belief in its integrity exists. Where this can be done, much more can be done on the same basis.

What are the problems that face these progressive and reform-minded persons? A Westerner will discover many of them as his experience in the Middle East grows. In Tehran, in 1946, I reviewed a preliminary report dealing with a vaguely proposed seven-year plan. It had been prepared mainly by a distinguished ex-cabinet minister of the reformer type, with European degrees in both law and economics. As it was worked over by the politicians, however, the social objectives were dropped out, and a memorandum transmitting it to a legislative committee explained this by saying that, although social objectives had merit, not everything could be done at once and, obviously, economic progress was more important than social reforms.

In many situations a logical case can be made for concentrating first upon the economic aspects of development, to provide the means for social improvement. In this case, however, an abundance of funds from the then prosperous oil industry would seem, to most Westerners, reason enough for giving priority to the development of much-needed human resources, and at the same time bringing prompt relief to a long-suffering population. The decision in this case was not based upon that kind of logic. Among the Persians at the decision-making level, the priority of economic over social development was not a matter of opinion but of accepted fact. That ninety percent of the population was illiterate, and living at or near a subsistence level, seemed to them a natural state. They might agree that this was an unenviable destiny for those born to it, but they could not take their eyes off the swift and shiny road to modernization of the country through building factories and mechanizing farming operations. They did not stop to ponder the questions of who would operate the factories, where the purchasing power to buy their output would come from, or how agricultural machinery would be maintained.

The very sincerity of this attitude is what baffles the Westerner, at least the American. I could never get used to hearing them tell casually about how many villages they had bought or sold, realizing that this is exactly what they meant —villages, body and soul, for all practical purposes, just as we would buy acres of land. My friends argued patiently with me that they took good care of their peasants, and in general I would say that they did—in the same sense that my own father used to take good care of his cattle. If the peasants were left on their own, it was said, many would starve, and so would others dependent upon their production for food. Strangely, this conviction was not confined to the elite but persisted, with variations, at other levels. Salaried employees and shop-owners, for example, would scrape their savings together and buy a village or two, and would often treat the peasants more harshly than the aristocrat who owned two or three hundred villages. Even the peasants themselves, except when aroused, seemed to accept their servile status as natural. These attitudes are part of the problem that faces the reformers. If people really believe that what they are doing is the natural thing to do, change must begin in them.

Class attitudes and distinctions also produce other problems. My own first efforts to create a conventional engineering department in Persia, and to make preliminary studies before the organization of the first Seven-Year Plan had been set up, I found to be wrong from the start, although I didn't know why. On the whole the men I was dealing with were first class in both character and professional training. I took pride in my association with them. But my idea of having a chief engineer and assistant, eight or ten functional sections each with its own supervisor, and appropriate subdivisions simply did not work. Both morale and group output were low. I took this up with the ones I knew best and quickly got my answer.

In selecting men for particular posts, according to their training and experience, I had disregarded the relative standing of their families, and therefore had produced some intolerable inversions of status. I called the leading group together, with due care to their selection this time, and asked them if they would give me their own idea of an organization that would produce the results which I specified as essential, such as delegation of responsibility and authority, coordination, effective use of specialists, and so on. To this they agreed. The following day we met again, and I could see success in their faces. Their organization chart, when they spread it out, consisted of one long horizontal line from which were suspended twenty or more named positions evenly across the chart, with one chief engineer above the middle of the line. No name appeared in this space. When I had recovered from my first reaction, I asked weakly, "How will you ever agree on a chief engineer?" Several answered at once: "We will elect him every six months!" Believe it or not, their plan worked—with only one modification. I drew the line at the election of a chief engineer, but agreement was reached on one man who had both professional and social qualifications. Why the rest of it worked as well as it did, I never found out. I am sure that it would not have at home. Friends who have lived in Japan have told me that they have seen somewhat the same thing there—weird organizational anomalies that somehow work faultlessly but cause American "experts" to shake their heads in disbelief.

Some years earlier I encountered this prestige factor in another setting. A wealthy Turkish agriculturalist had responded to the urge to expand into the industrial field and, using a German contractor, had built a modern iron foundry on the outskirts of Istanbul. If there was anything that Turkey needed at that time it was just such an iron foundry. Nevertheless, within a year or so it was bankrupt, and I was invited to diagnose and prescribe. The plant was ideally equipped and all in perfect condition, and the workmen appeared to be competent. The market was clamoring for cast-iron parts, and there was no local competition. The books were well kept— but there were no sales. In walking around the yard I noticed a number of large bronze propellers, obviously defective, in various stages of being cut up for scrap, and asked where they came from. The owner replied, "That's what we make, bronze propellers, large ones, for ships, big ships." Though I was by no means an expert in this field, I did know that bronze propellers—large ones, for ships, big ships—were a highly specialized product even in European foundries. And besides, there was no demand for them in Istanbul. I mentioned this and asked why he was not instead turning out tons of brake shoes and car wheels for the state railway, and cooking-pots, wagon and plow parts, and cheap tools for the local bazaar. "That is ironmonger's work," he replied simply. "You must remember my family's position!"

In recent years, however, all through the Middle East, the conspicuous factor of "prestige"—as the term is loosely used —seems to have been diminishing in importance in the private sector of the economy. This is, perhaps, largely because a steadily increasing part of private business is being developed by middle-class entrepreneurs instead of by traditionally elite classes, and middle-class businessmen are less concerned with prestige than with profit. It may also be because even among the socially elite, the acquisition of wealth creates a prestige of its own that competes with mere genealogical luster. A member of one of the most lustrous families in Persia added to his already considerable fortune by the manufacture and sale of Mickey Mast—a "jazzed-up" version of the traditional *mast* (yogurt, or clabbered milk). This drink was popularized through an amusing "Mickey Mouse" symbol, and marketed with a zest more suggestive of American bally-hoo than of aristocratic Persian lineage.

One of the most striking illustrations of the prestige motive is the attitude toward steel mills. It has often been observed that in the eyes of newly developing countries a steel mill seems to mark the coming of age—the proof that moderniza-tion has been achieved. Now it is true that there is a time, in a certain combination of circumstances, when a steel mill may warrant high priority, but this time is nearly always long after steel plows, wheelbarrows, nails, bolts, and other simple implements have begun to be manufactured within the country. Some countries, however, demand their own steel mills before steel plows and wheelbarrows are even being used, much less manufactured. Turkey's steel mill at Karabuk, built by Ataturk, is an example. It was a deadweight on the Turkish economy from the beginning. It absorbed practically the full capacity of a single-track railway to supply it with ore from the iron mines six hundred miles away and with coal from Zonguldak seventy-five miles in the other direction. It also absorbed most of the technical skill of the country, and most of the profits made by other state-operated undertakings. As an economic white elephant it would be hard to match—although Reza Shah attempted to match it in Persia until the war interrupted the attempt. The Persian undertaking has been revived, with American help, and an even greater eco-nomic travesty may be produced. What is there about a steel mill that makes people want one in a country that has not yet equipped itself to manufacture even the simplest agricultural machinery?

The propensity for erecting ostentatious public buildings also raises a similar question. They are everywhere. During the height of the unrest in Azerbaijan in 1949, with the peasants at the point of revolt, a lavish new palace was built for the governor with complete disregard for the hovels and other marks of destitution around it. Reza Shah's half-built opera house in Tehran, abandoned because its inadequate foundations gave way, held a lesson that was never learned by its builder—nor has it been learned by those who, more recently, built an imposing Senate Building, more impressive than the institution it houses. And in the Arab countries to the south, examples also abound. Ornate palaces for Arab princes and shaikhs, and expensive automobiles that are unsuited for desert use and last only until the crankcase runs dry of oil, are commonplace. But ostentatious show-places cannot always be traced to prestige-seeking. In Baghdad, a railway station, built at a cost of a million pounds sterling half a mile from the railway to Basrah that it was intended to serve (once described by an honest Englishman as "two streaks of rust across the desert"), can be explained more easily, at least in part, by the interests of the British contractors who built it.

Steel mills and monumental buildings can perhaps be explained as manifestations of a need to exhibit superiority, or if not to exhibit it, at least to feel it. Of course, they also serve the self-interests of a few, but the satisfaction in showy projects frequently is shared even by those whose own interests have been sacrificed. Thus a shopkeeper in the local bazaar will beam with pride at the new steel mill, although he will continue to pound out his hand-wrought nails from old bits of scrap iron, and mend his roof with gasoline tins. It does not occur to him that if even a small part of that vast expenditure had been devoted to the rehabilitation of shops like his throughout the country, supplying them with tools, material, and training, it would have provided much more tangible satisfactions both for the shopkeepers and for the masses they serve.

Sooner or later this will be pointed out, either by popular reform leaders or by subversive propaganda. In Bahrain when a modern power plant was built in the growing city of Manama, miles of shining steel towers carried transmission lines to supply distant peasant and fishing villages with electricity for the first time. Relative to the economy of the country, the cost of this project was high, although it was paid for by oil revenues (there are no taxes in Bahrain). When the substation in each village was switched on with pomp and ceremonial speeches, the villagers cheered and celebrated the blaze of lights festooned around the substation. The lights were then moved on to the next village where the ceremony was repeated, and the villagers—who traditionally went to bed shortly after sundown—were left in the dark as before. This took place in Bahrain during the rebellious years 1954–1957, and the popular leaders of the rebellion made a strong issue of the allocation of funds to an expensive transmission system—or to the British contractors who built it—instead of to local water wells, more schools, and land and agricultural development. The satisfaction first felt, of belonging to a village that was supplied with electricity, soon changed to anger. Such a change can take place very quickly, especially when aided by purposeful propaganda.

It is not easy for a Western visitor to the Middle East to find out, by direct observation, what the people do want or why they want it. This is particularly true when he leaves the main centers, with their elite groups and businessmen—whose motivations can at least be reasonably conjectured—and gets closer to the people themselves. Even before leaving the cities he will be close to some of them—low-salaried office workers, shopkeepers, hand-craft artisans of many kinds, itinerant laborers and their families. In the larger cities must be added the students—a separate category because their age-group characteristics, including a volatile condition of mind, make their behavior unique. All the Middle East cities afford evidence of a trend that seems to be worldwide: people moving from rural areas to the urban centers. It is among these town and city fringe populations that most subversive movements are started, and that most violent riots take place. Employment is scarce and there is leisure for listening to rabble-rousers. The traditional restraints of village or tribal communities do not exist in the cities. This complex of factors makes it difficult to find any pattern of behavior.

Away from the cities, the Middle East is a different world, a village and tribal world in which around eighty percent of the people live. One of the first things to strike a Westerner's attention as he moves through the country is that he never sees a dwelling standing alone with a field or farm around it. I have often wondered what the villagers of the Middle East would think if they saw America, where from coast to coast every farm has its farmhouse, and the village consists mainly of shops. Throughout the Middle East a building standing alone in the countryside is almost invariably a police station, or in recent years, a schoolhouse. The people live in clusters of huts almost indistinguishable from the hillside against which they are placed. From these crowded quarters they go out at daybreak to work in fields within ox-walking distance, or to tend their flocks, and return at dusk to the security of their community. Typically, outside the main cities, the Middle East seems empty, with small and scattered concentrations of families, each settlement independent of the rest and separated by an expanse of uninhabited and unused land. Only in recent years have country roads begun to be built to connect them. Donkey paths have met all their needs.

Paradoxically, it is in Saudi Arabia, with its vast oceans of sand and barren gravel plains, that I have found the greatest dispersion of people over the countryside. In 1937, with three companions, I made a thousand-mile trek across that country from the Persian Gulf to Jiddah on the Red Sea. We traveled for hours along an ancient mile-wide caravan route, marked by camel skeletons and other evidences of long use, without seeing a sign of humanity. But almost invariably when we stopped for a rest and some coffee, within minutes a *bedu* would appear from nowhere, and after the customary exchange of greetings, would join us around our fire. Within half an hour the chances were good that another half-dozen would appear. In little more time than it takes to tell it, they would start a small fire of camel dung in a hole scooped out in the sand (disdaining our own larger blaze) and roast a few coffee beans, which they then pounded together with cardamum seed and boiled with not much more than an ordinary cupful of water in a long-spouted coffee pot. This served the company with tiny cups of pungent brew, strained through the grass (we always hoped it was grass) packed in the pelican-like spout. After this brief ceremony, and farewells, we would be on our way, and long before the camp was out of sight our friends had disappeared.

An untrained eye in the desert misses many things that are there and sees many others that are not. Even a camel, unless on the skyline, may not be noticed until it is close by. The combination of heat and light plays strange tricks. On another trek into the western desert of Egypt, my companions and I left our car and trudged off toward a hill surmounted by a tower, apparently a mile or so away, from which we hoped to get a better view of the terrain. In a couple of minutes the hill and its tower came to meet us with a rush. What snapped into view was a discarded oil drum on a low sand dune, a few hundred feet from where we started.

But it is not only heat and light that play strange tricks on Western senses. The real difficulty lies in recognizing the ways in which Middle Easterners are different from us in the

West, and the ways in which they are the same. Children, outside the cities and towns, and to some extent even in them, display the same extremes of shyness and affectionate confidence in strangers that they do everywhere else in the world. Among adults, too, friendships across cultures and even across language barriers are easily formed. Before my wife knew a word of Arabic (she never studied Turkish or Persian), she formed friendships that have lasted through the years with families that spoke only those languages. Although interpreters are sometimes essential, my wife could commune, if not communicate, with these people. The knitting or sewing in their laps, a child playing on the floor near them, and a firm clasping of hands at parting can establish an understanding not only deeper but safer than gossip. And interpreters do not always interpret; sometimes they only translate. At one such meeting between Arab *shaikhas* and some Americans including my wife, one of the Arab ladies asked an American mother how her little girl had liked a sweater that had been knitted for her. The mother replied, in the American way, that the little girl had been tickled to death with it. When this was translated, the Arab ladies lifted their hands in horror—until a missionary wife, laughing herself to tears, put the matter right. What the translater had said was, "it scratched her until she died!"

As a Westerner settles himself into an Arab community and begins to think of the people he sees every day as individuals, with names, families, and problems of their own, he is constantly reminded that their ways are not ours, and that the differences may be deeper than he thought. The necessary accommodation to their ways is not simple.

By accommodating to their ways I do not mean in the manner of those bearded and barefooted Western characters who "go native." Such condescending antics are more likely to affront than to please. Twenty years or more ago there were good reasons for Western visitors to wear Arab dress in certain circumstances, for example when traveling in the interior, or when calling upon Arab notables. In such cases suitable Arab garments—*abbah, thoub,* and *khafiyah*—were commonly gifts to the visitor, to be used for the occasion. Today there are few situations where such dress is necessary— or even appropriate. At least some among the Arab hosts are likely to be wearing European clothes themselves.

The adjustment that must be made to their ways is in the mind, and the spirit in which one seeks to understand them. Without this adjustment, Westerners are likely to write them down as ignorant, superstitious, or even savage. I can illustrate this with an experience of my own.

In the early days of the American oil company in Bahrain, I had much to do with the patriarchal Ruler of that time. He made our son and me the gift of the Island of Umm A'Sabaan, for a home of our own in his domain. In his simple, straightforward manner and his love of well-bred animals he reminded me of my own father, who would have been about the same age. I sat with him many times, with or without an interpreter, near the door of his hunting lodge at Romaitha— a pavilion affording shelter from the sun in the uninhabited part of Bahrain Island—while his favorite horses and camels were led past for inspection, and for his comments on their meritorious points.

One day a sailing *dhow* with three men aboard was found drifting by local fishermen and brought to port in Bahrain. Both eyes of two of the men had been burned out with hot irons. The third had been spared one eye for navigation. They were treated by the oil company doctor. It was learned that they had come from one of the Trucial Shaikhdoms further south, the so-called Pirate Coast, where they had been punished for an alleged conspiracy against their local shaikh. When I had an opportunity I asked our Ruler if he did not consider the punishment overly severe. After reflection he answered, "No. You see, maybe they were guilty." At such times as this his resemblance to my own father faded.

All Westerners who have worked in the Middle East know how difficult it is to change practices that have become fixed by tradition. All of them, too, have been astonished by the suddenness with which change sometimes takes place. The perplexing thing is to know which way it is going to be. The only safe assumption, at least to begin with, is that nothing that is done there will have the same results as it would at home. One might think that nothing could be simpler than demonstrating to a practical farmer that, by following a certain procedure in seed selection and use of water, fertilizer, and so on, a better and more abundant crop will result. In a surprising number of cases, nevertheless, such a demonstration will be set aside with the comment that this is not the way it is done by them.

It took us ten years, in our own garden in Umm A'Sabaan, to persuade our Arab gardeners that leaves and grass put to rot in a compost pit would produce a valuable *samad* (fertilizer). Year after year, despite the visible effects of this samad when we were there to insist upon its production and use, our hard-won heaps would be burned as soon as we would turn our backs, and the ashes spread over the garden in the time-honored way. But one year when we returned from an absence, we found that our gardeners had energetically converted nearly everything growing on the island, including our vegetable and flower beds, into compost. They explained the virtues of this new samad to us as though we were hearing of it for the first time.

I suspect that many Middle East traditions had a basis in experience at some time and place. Thus the objection to compost may have originated in an area where the soil was naturally heavy with organic material and deficient in the minerals supplied by the ashes; or the burning of the dead leaves may have been a practical way to kill pest life each season, before insecticides became available, although I never heard these reasons given.

Where basic concepts concerning plant growth are lacking (and Westerners sometimes forget how many simple facts concerning such things are known even by our children in the West), verbal explanations as to why certain practices should be followed are useless. Even demonstrations are set aside with the argument that, if Allah wills, anyone may get such results once in a while.

The lack of understanding of how plants grow, how disease is spread, and how simple machines work—in the ordinary terms of elementary biology, chemistry, and physics—is a barrier to the introduction of new ways, because no reason for a changed practice can be given that is better than their own reasons for rejecting it.

One time I made a stop on the land of a small but obviously progressive farmer in southern Turkey. He spoke fair English, and he invited me to have a look at a new pump that he had recently installed. It was to supply water to an extension of his land too high for his canal system to irrigate. His pride in his pump was justified. It was a centrifugal pump of modern design, driven by a small diesel engine and mounted beside a new concrete basin from which the water flowed by gravity into the pump. The basin, however, was kept full of water by means of an immense wooden wheel, with buckets around its edges, dipping into the spring. The bucket wheel was turned by a creaking mechanism energized by two oxen, patiently milling around in a rut that was worn almost shoulder deep. The water in the spring was less than ten feet from the surface, and I asked the farmer why he did not simply drop the suction pipe of the pump into it, with a foot-valve on the end, and let the engine and pump do all the work, so he could use the oxen elsewhere. He rejected the suggestion as unworkable, even when I explained that, as a young engineer, I had designed such pumps myself and was familiar with them. No, he insisted; pumps could not make water come to them, they could only make water go away. I left with the satisfaction of knowing that he had a welcome surprise coming to him some day, and that meanwhile his needs were being met.

We cannot take the same satisfaction in cases where lack of understanding results in widespread suffering, or still worse, where lack of understanding on the part of some people means suffering for all, as in the case of simple improvements in sanitation, and the use of prophylactics for the control of endemic or contagious diseases. The Middle East peoples have always taken their own countermeasures against recognized diseases; they have no more desire to be sick than anyone else. But if they cannot associate cause with effect, or if their traditions associate disease with the wrong cause, the remedies that we offer may have no appeal.

As in the case of agricultural improvements, demonstrations may not be convincing; many sick people have got well using their own remedies, and those using ours do not live forever. Here, very often, there is need for compulsory measures. Vaccination against smallpox has required more police than doctors nearly everywhere, because a swollen and painful arm and a passing fever have little attraction compared to a rag flown over the housetop, or an incantation from the Koran, to accomplish the same purpose. Easier success with DDT for malarial control was due to the fact that this treatment killed fleas and lice—not to any relation between it and a reduction in fever cases months later. Typhoid is more difficult again, because of the prevalent belief, for which the Koran gives some ground, that running water is safe to drink —but there are many ways to make water run that do not purify it.

The compulsory use of sanitary latrines is also a matter for the police, even after latrines have been provided. Therapy for trachoma is long and painful, by present methods, and futile unless measures are taken to eliminate the prevailing filth and flies that bring prompt reinfection. Public baths that serve also as social meeting places are usually sinks of contagion, but the social function is not served at all by shower baths, however sanitary.

The use of police or other means of enforcing legislation aimed at public health or other social reforms presupposes a government that, first of all, cares about these things, and second, that is capable of creating the institutions and taking the measures that are necessary to make their programs effective. There is a propensity among Middle East government officials, quite generally, to make too little distinction between talking about doing something, or even deciding that it must be done, and actually doing it. To pass laws, for example, against child labor, or for compulsory attendance at school, or for a public health measure, is very likely to leave a government content that it has done its duty.

As an illustration, in connection with Persia's first Seven-Year Plan an eminent constitutional lawyer was brought from New York to review the procedures of the Majlis as a legislative body. His informal report stated that he had found on their books every law that he had ever heard of—but not one that was being enforced.

But there are different ways to enforce laws. When an American-trained Persian physician accepted the post of Minister of Health under the Razmara regime, among the acute problems facing him was that of ridding Tehran of its quack doctors and pharmacists, whose practices were shameful even by local standards. So many laws were on the books, however, touching the matter of licenses for various kinds of health treatment, that local lawyers were able to erect legal defenses around these quacks. Finally the hard-hitting Minister became desperate. One morning he took a large lorry and a squad of gendarmes, went down one street and up the next, collecting the protesting charlatans, and took fifteen or twenty of them to jail. The rest quickly pulled in their signs, but those apprehended set up an immediate clamor and demanded to be shown under what law they had been arrested. The Minister's answer was prompt. "You are now in jail," he told them grimly. "You show me the law that says you can get out!"

The Western visitor to the Middle East, confronted with so many patterns of behavior, may conclude that the Middle East is so different from the West that it is hard to think of either society in terms that apply to the other. And despite many characteristics that are common among large groups of Middle East peoples, their society as a whole presents a wider range between extremes of many kinds—social, cultural, political, and economic—than is found in Western countries. But the conclusion likely to be the most significant is that everything that he has seen is changing. Even many of the differences among the peoples he has observed seem to reflect different degrees of change along a prevailing trend, rather than differences inherent in the people themselves.

Chapter Three

Social Institutions

TRADITIONALLY, the basic social institution in the Middle East has been the family. One of the most significant changes that has taken place in recent years has been in this fundamental unit, and particularly in the *extended family*, which consists of all the members identified by a given patrilineal descent. The extended family, which gave the traditional society one of its most important structural features, has been fast disintegrating. The more remote degrees of relationship that through long custom delimited a kinship group as a tribe have in some circumstances proved less binding than the ties with other groups that have been formed outside the family. Wherever this has happened, the extended family has tended progressively to shrink to the two, three, or four generations of the same paternal line that live together under one roof, submit to the same senior authority in family affairs, jointly safeguard the family honor, and share together the burdens and blessings of life. Even the basic parent-child relationship is swinging toward the pattern familiar in the West, with the younger generation claiming increasing independence as soon as adolescence is reached—and even before.

The reasons for this weakening of family ties—or at least, some circumstances under which it seems to take place—are readily seen. New ideas of many kinds have been introduced through new media of communications, and they moderate older cultural and social ways. Migrations from rural to urban surroundings have removed many traditional restraints that exist in village life but are lost or replaced by different ones in city life. Technological innovations provide opportunities for youths with schooling that are not open to the generally illiterate older generation. These opportunities not only take the younger group away from the family circle but introduce an economic factor as well. The youth of sixteen or eighteen, that is, may earn three or four times as much as his father. A young man in farming may produce a surplus over subsistence, for the market, because of his knowledge of improved methods. Such capabilities have changed his status within the family, and have increased his independence.

In the older tradition, the most significant break with family ways was likely to occur when a man succeeded to his father's place and began to exercise his new authority by making the adjustments necessary to relieve stresses that had been built up by cumulative restraints and new influences. Thereafter he might become as conservative toward further change as his father had been before him. For many centuries in the Middle East, periodic change of this kind was minor. In Egypt, Turkey, Persia, and a few of the Arab countries it began to be more noticeable after the First World War, partly under foreign influences. In some of the Arab countries it can scarcely be noticed even yet; in others it is just beginning.

In Bahrain, the long line of traditional rulers had seen no reason for changing anything, until Shaikh Hamad acceded in 1923. He introduced some innovations that he recognized were due, and thereafter remained content. His son Shaikh Sulman, on his accession in 1942, also set things right as he saw them, but in recent years recognized little further necessity for disturbing a reasonably satisfactory order. It seems likely that under his son Shaikh Isa, a young man with wide foreign travel, substantial changes will again be made in adjustment to the times.

Mohammed Reza, Shah-in-shah of Persia, in his recent autobiography, made a strong point of his own departure from his father's ways.* This same generation-by-generation adjustment in viewpoints is clearly seen in the policies of many merchant families. In the masses, too, it seems reasonable to suppose that the step-by-step change from father to son still takes place, but here the shift in authority cannot be so easily watched. But what is conspicuous among the younger age groups today is that they are no longer waiting to succeed to authority before adjusting to new ideas and influences.

This breaking down of the traditional family is hastened by the same factors that are accelerating social and economic change. It need not be argued here whether this is a social gain or loss; without doubt it is the prevailing trend. But a closer knowledge of what is happening to the family institution in different segments of Middle East society, and what brings the change about, would add greatly to Western understanding of other changes that are taking place. In many regions, where circumstances have not produced new groupings that were strong enough to dismember the extended family, there still exist large tribal units, bound together by at least a tradition of common lineage. Thus nearly the entire population of Saudi Arabia is characterized by its tribal structure, as is most of the rural population in the other Arab countries, except Egypt. Although census figures are deficient, probably nearly one-third of the total population of Persia is

* *Mission for My Country.* New York: McGraw-Hill, 1961, p. 44.

tribal. To what extent a tribal social structure still exists in Turkey is difficult for an outside observer to estimate.

A casual observer meeting tribes in such places as Saudi Arabia, the desert and mountain regions of Iraq, and western and southern Persia, may have trouble detecting what one tribe has in common with another except their primitive way of life, generally unkempt appearance, and wariness toward strangers. Some are wandering nomads, others make regular seasonal migrations, and still others live in permanently settled villages. A closer look at the circumstances in each case, however, begins to explain most of the differences, and if these variables are subtracted, the tribe emerges as a basic institution of society.

Generally speaking, this institution has distinctive attitudes toward the traditions of kinship, authority, personal rights and obligations, and many other aspects of social behavior. These attitudes clearly differentiate tribal from typical village or urban society. It is particularly important to understand what happens when tribal institutions come into conflict with other institutions—for example, with the allocation of rights to land, water, or travel routes as established by modern laws, or more generally, with the political authority of a central government. In such collisions it must not be assumed that tribal members will behave simply like "people"; they will behave like people to whom certain ways of behaving have become institutionalized. And before those ways can undergo change the institution itself must undergo change.

General Razmara, while Chief of Staff of the Persian military forces, once told me that to govern Persia one must know the tribes, and he had compiled an encyclopedia of factual data concerning them, although the conventional political authority of the central government, or even the gendarmerie, was seldom exercised inside the tribal areas. The success of the British in maintaining the tolerable state of order in the areas bordering the Persian Gulf for more than two hundred years rested largely upon their understanding of tribal ways. And when, more than a century ago, control of this region became essential to the security of the British "life line," the earliest published reports of the British India Government concerning the region dealt with tribal organization and customs—not with economic resources, geography, or history. For thirty years Ibn Saud ruled his desert Kingdom of Saudi Arabia, with its highly dispersed population, through the traditional mechanism of its tribal organization, which he understood well. Today the transition from that tribal organization to modern political, economic, and social institutions presents one of the most complex problems in social change in the Middle East.

The impact of modern upon tribal institutions is well illustrated by the introduction, in Iraq, of a system of recording land ownership. Some such system was a basic requirement for both taxation and investment for development. Ownership of tribal lands was recorded in the name of the paramount chief of the tribe. Later, as land was developed, the economic benefits accrued solely to the chief and his family, with the accumulation, in some cases, of very large fortunes, usually spent in lavish living by the family. Technically, this disposition of rights conformed with the rules of both the old and the new institutions, but the results destroyed the basis upon which the old institution rested. Along with other changes having similar effect, this contributed to the progressive disintegration of traditional society. The periodic uprisings of the tribal fellahin of southern Iraq against their absentee landlord chiefs, and the more recent rebellion of other tribes following the 1958 coup, have offered continuing evidence of the upheaval.

The village, as a social institution, is just as basic to the traditional society of the Middle East as the family and the tribe. Typical villages in the Middle East are not to be compared with a suburban village in the United States, in which a family merely finds it convenient to live for a time—perhaps even without knowing their neighbors. A traditional Middle East village, until comparatively recent influences from outside began to change it, was the only world its members knew. The cycle of birth, marriage, and death might go on for generations within it, or within a small group of neighboring villages.

Villages and village ways vary from region to region, and vary according to cultural, occupational, and other circumstances. Thus Turkish villages differ from Persian ones; and even within the same country and region, fishing villages differ from peasant villages, and from those of charcoal-burners, rug weavers, or potters. But the type of village most often seen in the Middle East by the Westerner is that of the peasant farmer. And the commonest type of peasant village, perhaps, is that in which a landlord owns the land, and the farming is done by the peasants on a sharecrop basis. Landlord-peasant relationships vary from region to region; what is generally uniform among them is that the share received by the peasant is just enough to keep him and his family alive. These sharing systems take into account, in an elementary way, the productive value of capital and the division of labor. Capital, in such an economy, may be represented by ownership of—or rights to the use of—land, water, oxen, and implements, and by specially acquired skills. The division of labor is usually fixed by tradition, which is slow to change. In Persia, where sharecropping is the rule, there are many local variations of a formula under which one-fifth of the crop goes to the supplier of each of the following: land, seed, water, labor, and oxen.* If the shares attaching to land, seed, and water go to the landlord, as they commonly do, and if labor's

---

* For a more detailed description of Persian culture and society, see A. K. S. Lambton, *Landlord and Peasant in Persia*. Royal Press, 1953.

and oxen's shares must be divided among the fifteen or twenty families which average, say, at least five members to the family, with no market for any surplus they produce, it is small wonder that peasants place a low value upon achievement beyond what it takes to stay alive.

The case is not always this bad. There are good landlords as well as bad ones. Peasants usually have grazing rights for their flocks, and the right to grow seasonal fruit or vegetables for exchange in the local market. There are also peasant farmers who hold land of their own under a variety of rights in different countries, and who are entitled to all they produce, subject of course to taxes. Such rights, however, often become so subdivided through generations of partitioning inheritance that the lands are mere patches between the mud walls or hedges that separate them. A dozen or so such patches may represent a single family's widely scattered holdings in the communal area. In such circumstances, the obstacles to introducing modern agricultural methods and implements scarcely need mention.

In a peasant-farmed grain-growing region the scene in a typical village at harvest time cannot have changed much since biblical days. In Azerbaijan, for example, toward the close of summer when the wheat has been harvested and the oxen-drawn sleds with smooth rocks fitted to their bottoms have made their last circle over the layers of wheat-laden hay, and the last crude forkful has been winnowed by tossing it for the separation of the chaff, the picture could be described better by an artist than by an agricultural economist. Beside the worn circle left by the treading oxen lie heaps of golden wheat, each cone topped by the tip of a stick that marks the height to which it must be raised. The slopes of the heaps are uniform, because the "angle of repose" of cured wheat is nearly enough a constant. Thus each heap represents a certain quantity, and the disposition of the heaps marks the shares belonging to the landlord, the tax collector, and the village.

Once while I paused by the roadside to appreciate the beauty of one of these scenes, I asked my driver why the small boy beating on a piece of tin with a stick to keep the birds away concentrated on a few heaps while the birds pecked hungrily at the rest. Smilingly, my driver invited me to a closer look. Each of the cones guarded by the boy had been stamped on its slopes with a wooden tablet, a sample of which I was shown later, deeply carved in the manner of a seal— or a Western cattle brand—which would have made detectable the removal of even a few grains of wheat from the pile. The landlord had put his seal on one set of heaps, the tax collector on another, and these piles were being guarded from pillage by hungry birds in order to avoid penalties against which the peasants had no recourse. The birds' share came from the peasants—an elementary form of retrogressive taxation.

By far the greatest number of Middle East farming villages are in the highlands of Persia, Turkey, and the northern Arab countries. Within a month after the harvest the snow begins to fall. The peasants' grain is stored in their huts, to be ground and baked into bread—their staple food for the winter. The oxen are put into their sheds, which are piled over and around with straw to be doled out at a rate that keeps the animals alive until spring. I have been told that the main reason for using oxen, instead of horses—which, with wheeled plows, could double the land cultivated in the same time—is that oxen will survive these conditions, whereas horses would not. I can attest that even oxen barely survive them.

One of the images that the Western observer takes with him to the Middle East is that of the Moslem. He is prepared to find a follower of the Prophet Mohammed worshiping

Allah and finding guidance in the Koran for both his spiritual and his secular life. The Westerner may or may not have deeply studied Islam as a religion, a philosophy of life, a code of social conduct, and a legal system. In any case, his preparation to look for the ways in which Islam has made its impact upon people's lives is likely to be superficial.

Very little that he sees in the Middle East will impress him as reflecting a powerful present-day religious force capable of reshaping Middle East society. He will indeed be impressed by the beauty of the more famous mosques and by the exquisitely illuminated Koranic manuscripts on display in libraries and museums, but these will seem to belong to the glories of the past. He will know that what he does see today has been molded by thirteen centuries of Islamic influence, but just what that influence is, and the extent to which it is still acting, are difficult questions that cannot be answered through observation alone.

I will not attempt to describe the religion of the Middle East in detail. Its doctrinal and philosophical concepts, its history, art, and literature are better described in other sources.* But it is both feasible and relevant to discuss some of the observable manifestations of Islam as a social force, mainly the "folk religion" of the common people, with the barest doctrinal background to give it a setting.

Certain characteristics of the Moslem religion make it a more conspicuous factor in the behavior of common people than Christianity is in the West. Much of the Koranic code was intended to have authority over social as well as spiritual affairs, and it is not always easy for the Westerner to distinguish the merely statutory from the spiritual elements. Nor is it always clear where the Moslem himself draws the line between them, or even—in some cases—that he draws a

---

* For a brief, authentic, and highly readable account of Islamic religion, see H. A. R. Gibb, *Mohammedanism*. London: Oxford University Press, 1949.

line. The faithfulness and freedom from self-consciousness with which Moslems commonly observe their rituals, such as the public performance of their daily prayers, and the frequency of Koranic quotations in their ordinary conversations, can lead to exaggerated ideas of the real force exerted by their religion upon their behavior. On the other hand, it is probably true that the influence of religion among the Middle East masses has been heightened by the sparsity of other interests, which in more sophisticated societies tend to crowd religion into the background except at times habitually set aside for thinking about it. Millions of people in the Middle East have never had much else to think about.

Even so, the mistake must not be made of assuming that all behavior met in the Middle East that differs from that of the West has religious origins or significance. Often it is due to circumstances common to Moslem and non-Moslem alike. For example, the Moslem and Christian segments of the Lebanese population, about equal in numbers, display many common characteristics, particularly those Moslems and Christians who suffer alike from poverty, illiteracy, and oppressive class distinctions. Even certain behavior that does have religious origins—in the sense that it expresses belief in a spiritual world ruled by an unknowable Divine Order, for which life on earth is merely a preparation—may be no different among Moslems from corresponding behavior among many other religious people. Islam, as interpreted to its followers, drew heavily upon Judaistic and Christian teachings. Furthermore, much that was already deeply rooted in the various cultures that embraced Islam, unless it was expressly excluded (for example, the worship of images) continued in the form of superstitions that are inextricably bound up with the folk religion of the masses. All Westerners who have lived among these peoples know how real, to them, are the "jinns" and the workings of the "Evil Eye," and how potent the safeguards and remedies.

The non-Moslem observer cannot escape the impression that to the illiterate masses of Moslem peoples the folk religion is little more than a set of blindly accepted symbols reminding them that suffering on earth has been preordained, and that rewards are reserved for the next life. This sense of fatalism, unquestionably, has had much to do with the characteristic resignation of the poorer classes to their lot. In the past it may have been a solace. But this is changing. The peasant who consoled himself on the loss of his crop in a dry year, or a year of pests, by attributing it to the "will of Allah," is likely to make a new appraisal when he finds out what an irrigating pump can do in times of drought, or insecticides against plant pests. He is learning today that it was not a punishing Allah who kept him for so long in misery—but his government, his landlord, or his own indolence and ignorance. He is finding out that the same *kismet* (fate) that predestined the drought and the pests is equally ready to predestine the pump and the insecticides, if the peasant can find a way to get them. The same is true in the treatment of disease.

The Westerner knows, too, that at the level of folk religion, whatever the sanctity in which the Koran is held as the revealed Word of God, its meaning must be obscure to many to whom the classical Arabic of the Koran is an otherwise unknown tongue. This is true for many millions in the Middle East (as elsewhere) who have no knowledge of Arabic, and to many millions of Arabs, for that matter, whose own dialects are of little help in understanding the only version of the Koran which tradition has permitted for more than a thousand years. In many Islamic countries the same tradition still prohibits the repeating of the teachings and prayers of the Faith except in the original language.

Even so, the Westerner is likely to decide that the folk religion is more understandable—even though he may not be able to explain it all—than some things that he sees among literate groups whose practices cannot be attributed to ignorance or superstition. The impression is widespread among Westerners that many of the injunctions of the Koran are commonly evaded at this higher social level by devising the thinnest of casuistries to legitimize some more convenient conduct. This observation applies even to orthodox members of the Faith. Since the same criticism could be made of the way Christians observe, or fail to observe, their own religious teachings, there would be no point in making this comment except for the fact that such Moslem practices have been widely misinterpreted by Westerners.

The principal reasons for such noticeable evasion, reasons which Westerners would do well to bear in mind, have been mentioned in an earlier context: first, the Koran, as well as the "traditions" (*hadith*) stemming from the Prophet, enjoins upon the Faithful certain rules of social conduct that are completely secular in character and in a practical world must be interpreted in a practical way; and second, the open display the Moslems make of their religious observances invites attention to deviations in actual behavior which would not otherwise be interpreted as having doctrinal significance. An illustration or two will make both points clear.

The late Major General David P. Barrows, after his experience in the Moroccan Riff rebellion some years ago, once related the following anecdote. After a hard day's campaigning, the Moslem officers with whom he was traveling poured their guest and themselves a liberal round of brandy. Each officer, before touching his glass to his lips, gravely dipped his little finger into it and shook one drop onto the sand. They explained to the General that they were adjured not to drink one drop of liquor—and this was that drop! There may have been a bit of leg-pulling here, for the Arabs are not without humor. But if it were a joke, it was their joke, which makes much the same point.

In Moslem countries the Koranic injunction to give alms to the poor imposes no burden upon the conscience of some rich men that cannot be dismissed by distributing, on appropriate occasions, a few of the smallest coins in use—and there are some very small ones indeed—or by contributing to the poor the remnants of a meal that are left over after the servants have fed on them. This is not to conclude that personal generosity, and even large-scale philanthropy, are any less common among Moslems than among others. Any such conclusion would be quite wrong. What catches the stranger's attention is the *pretext* that a religious duty has been performed, and he may wonder how many others are performed in the same perfunctory way.

The injunction against charging interest on loans has been evaded through the centuries, and continues to be evaded where Western practices have not yet taken hold. In bazaars throughout the Moslem world the evasion is accomplished through a simple device. The applicant for a loan "sells" a sack of rice (or some other commodity) to the money-lender for whatever amount is to be borrowed. At the same time he contracts to buy it back again on a certain date at an agreed-upon higher price. The difference represents the money-lender's profit on the transaction, but technically it is not classifiable as "interest." A single sack of rice standing by the money-lender's table may be tipped back and forth between buyers and sellers until it is worn out with use. "Sales profits" as high as twenty-five percent a month are not unusual for short-term loans—without technical violation of the Koranic rule. The introduction of Western-type commercial institutions, including banks, instalment buying, various agricultural and other credit agencies, and the like, has brought a growing acceptance of the principle that a reasonable charge for the use of capital may properly be made, and that the rule against interest, originally aimed at curbing rapacious money-lenders, need not be applied literally to modern business. But the Koranic injunction against interest is by no means a dead letter among devout Moslems. The Ruler of Bahrain contributed substantially from his own funds to provide capital for the Bank of Bahrain (a private institution) but with the distinct provision that no interest earned on its loans would be credited to his account. By reliable report the Ruler of Kuwait has made a similar stipulation concerning all loans from his own considerable capital to other Arab states.

The point of all this is that such palpable evasions as those just illustrated are not evidences of hypocrisy, but of the doctrinal dilemma which confronts the Moslem, but from which the Christian is spared. To Christians, the Word of God was revealed by Jesus acting as a divine instrument and the New Testament was the work of mortal men who, each in his own way, wrote of what Jesus had revealed. To Moslems, the divine instrument through which the Word of God was revealed was the Koran itself, not the Prophet Mohammed, whose part was simply that of a mortal transcriber. Thus from a doctrinal viewpoint the strictly orthodox Moslem is not free to tamper with the Word as received, even by translating it into another language. Where the Koran touches secular as distinguished from spiritual affairs, therefore, the Moslem has no recourse but to force the realities of modern life into a form that leaves the Word of God intact, even though this produces some apparent distortion of realities. The Christian is admonished to distinguish what is to be rendered unto Caesar from what is to be rendered unto God. The Moslem, although spared, in respect to Mohammed, many of the perplexities that the divinity of Jesus might raise in doubting minds, has been left with far less freedom than the Christian to decide what is to be rendered unto Caesar and what unto

God, and whether what was due Caesar in the seventh century is still due him today.

The Westerner with long residence among Moslem friends is likely to revise his pre-formed image in still another way. Despite the differences between the Moslem and Christian modes of divine revelation, there is a great deal of similarity in what was revealed. Such a judgment is necessarily a subjective one but at least it rests upon some empirical evidence. The best evidence that I can give is that among my own close Moslem and Christian friends, those whose lives have come the closest to exemplifying the principles of their respective faiths have also come the closest in resemblance to each other.

From what the observer sees around him throughout the Middle East it is obvious that many changes have taken place in the practice of Islam since the Koran was first revealed to the Prophet and interpreted by the early caliphs. Evidence of this on the doctrinal side is seen, for example, in the diversity of sects into which the Moslems have become divided. The origins and evolution of these schisms, and of other controversies that have produced an ebb and flow of rival doctrines down through the centuries, have been traced by Islamic scholars. Some of the highlights are sketched in the section on legal systems, below, a subject to which those schisms have relevance. There are other aspects of change in Islam, however, that need mentioning here because of their importance in contemporary Middle East affairs.

One aspect is the evolutionary revision of doctrine which marks Islam as a living religion, and which proceeds slowly under the devout guidance of Islamic scholars (the *ulema*) to keep the revealed Message meaningful in a changing society. Another is an ecological adaptation of the secular injunctions of the Koran and its supplementary sources of Islamic law, to suit the new conditions under which human conduct requires regulation in the public interest. The "revisionist movement" applies to all Islam, although it is not uniform among all sects. The second trend, ecological change, is more strongly affected by national and local developments.

Ecological change is simply adaptation to changed environment, and most environmental changes in the Middle East today are related closely to national affairs. Thus the revolutions in Turkey and Persia that were led by Ataturk and Reza Shah produced radical political and economic changes which necessitated many breaks with traditional institutions, religious practices, and the status of religious leaders among them. Indeed, the increasing elaboration of political and economic systems as dominant characteristics of a society quite generally have this effect. At the same time, technological innovations tend to diminish the uncertainties of crop production and treatment of disease, and thus gradually erode the fatalistic attribution of all forms of adversity to supernatural causes.

For these reasons the widely disparate impacts of Islam upon society as between, say, Saudi Arabia or Yemen on the one hand and Turkey or Egypt on the other, are not deviations from some early norm of Islamic doctrine due solely to conflicting interpretations of dogma. To a considerable extent they reflect also the degree of social, political, and economic sophistication of those societies. This being so, the expectation follows that somewhat similar disparities will be found within a single country in which social stratification has produced a similar range of sophistication. As a matter of fact, just such differences in religious attitudes are frequently found in the Middle East.

There is another way in which the influence of Islam upon social behavior has at least been under pressure toward change: a way which has considerable contemporary significance. For many centuries Islam was faced with two main contests, an internal one against the forces of evil, and an external one against rival religious faiths, both resting upon doctrinal grounds. But Moslems, like all other peoples, now live in an age in which secular ideologies—democracy, nationalism, and Communism among others—not only contest among themselves but contest with religion for a hold upon men's minds. Even the most militant religious faiths have lost ground to secular ideologies, and Islam, realistically speaking, is no longer militant. Although no doctrinal change is involved, in relation to rival influences Islam as a spiritual force now faces crucial attrition. The most imminent threat is that as a force governing human behavior it will be supplanted by Communist ideology. This threat faces other religious faiths also, but is made more explicit in the case of Islam by the basic doctrinal concept of *jihad,* through which the Koran enjoins every Moslem to preserve the Way of God against all dangers.

Western writers commonly give an erroneous meaning to *jihad* through its translation as "holy war," with the implication that *jihad* is limited to actual fighting between armed forces of Moslems and "infidels"—as, for example, in the wars of the Crusades. On the contrary, *jihad* seldom takes this form, although it may. More often it simply expresses the struggle, within Islam itself or even within an individual, to maintain the Way of God, as revealed by the Koran, against heresy or defection.

The increasing secularization of political and social affairs within Islamic countries progressively diminishes the likelihood that *jihad* will express itself in actual war. The conditions that could make such *jihad* possible, even on a limited scale, appear to exist only within a few fanatical communities found in Moslem Africa and a few isolated parts of the Middle East. Even in these cases, the absence of any overt external threats to Islam, based solely on religious issues, would probably cut short any militant fervor that could be stirred up by religious exhortation. The Crusades are over, and the wars that have been fought in modern times have had very different, if not more elevated, origins. It is true, of course, that there exist religious groups that are predisposed to fanatical and violent expressions of the moods excited in them by their leaders. Even within the last few years there have been notable exhibitions of such moods. But despite the fact that the group itself has been held together by some common religious affinity, the objectives toward which its fury was directed have not been religious objectives. Therefore they could not generate such supplies of spiritual exaltation as sustained Saladin's campaigns against the Christian Crusaders.

The *mullah* Kashani was such a religious group leader in the early days of Mossadegh's rebellion in Persia; but Kashani led his followers against the Shah, the British, the oil company, and finally against Mossadegh himself. There was evidence of repeated efforts on the part of Kashani's lieutenants to turn this onslaught into a holy war. But *jihads* are not fought against oil companies or politicians as such, and the movement soon assumed its proper character as a popular demonstration against unpopular institutions.

The case of Kashani illustrates the important point that a group strongly fastened together and to its leader by any sort of tie becomes a tactical unit capable of exerting a united effort toward whatever end may be designated by its leader. This might be true of such organizations as the Moslem Brotherhood, the Arab League, or the followers attached to King Saud as Head of the Wahabi Sect and the Protector of the Holy Cities (Mecca and Medina). In such cases, however, the strength of the group would lie in its mechanism for effective tactical direction, not in its spiritual character.

Despite the specters raised from time to time by Western journalists, a "holy war" in our times is to be expected only in the unlikely event that the Faithful are called upon to protect Islam against the unbeliever. As well as one can judge today's chief concerns, both the Faithful and the unbelievers are more interested in political rivalries, oil concessions, air and naval bases, and the price of a loaf of bread.

There is, nevertheless, a possibility that conflicts between contemporary ideologies may develop into conflicts involving religious principles. Much has been said in recent years, particularly by Western writers, about the possibility of conflict between Communism and Islam. Realistically, the question must be viewed as involving both doctrinal issues and issues of a pragmatic character arising from the impact of Communism, as it appears to Islamic masses, upon their folk religion. The types of issues raised may be quite different in the two cases, although the distinction is not always made by Westerners.

One widespread opinion has been expressed by Professor Edward S. Mason, of Harvard University, as follows.

To most of the religious people of the area [southeast Asia] whether Moslem, Hindu, Buddhist, or other, the communist doctrine of the totalitarian state with its relation of the government to the people is abhorrent. In southeast Asia as elsewhere religion is a strong bulwark against communism.*

Opposed to this is another view, to which the author inclines—although not with absolute conviction—namely, that Communism could find no more fertile field than that provided by Islam, particularly an Islam which has become decadent and uninspired. Thus S. A. Morrison, after a lifetime of close association in church work with Moslems, says, "The common conception that because communist atheism and Islamic belief in the all-powerful will of God are incompatible . . . communism cannot take hold in Moslem countries, is founded on a grave misreading of the situation." †

---

* Edward S. Mason, *Economic Planning in Underdeveloped Areas.* New York: Fordham University Press, 1958.
† This and the following two quotations are from S. A. Morrison, *Middle East Tensions.* New York: Harper & Brothers, 1954.

Morrison goes on to quote Albert Hourani as saying:

Communism can spread among those on whom the inherited religion has lost its hold, and it can spread even within the framework of Islam. It is quite compatible with vague "religiosity"—Muslim no less than Christian—and its conception of society has points in common with that of Islam. Both are conceptions of a universal society based on equality, and striving toward social justice; both think of reform in terms of cataclysm, the sudden change which will make all things new; in both social idealism goes together with moral protest against the laxity of the world.

Morrison also refers to other characteristic features that are common to both systems:

Their totalitarian doctrine, their fanaticism and collectivism, their division of the world into two sectors, their sense of mission, their concept of a community of believers which is always in the right, and finally their dependence on the state to control economic life.

The opposing views just indicated strike at deeper qualities than can be observed by the casual witness of everyday behavior. Westerners, nevertheless, would do well to be cautious in their acceptance of Islam as a first line of defense against Communism. Communism may be atheistic but Communist agents in Moslem countries do not preach atheism to Moslems. Moreover, the fact that there are many millions of Moslems living within the Communist borders, though it may not prove the point, certainly suggests that Moslems might be produced in abundance to persuade other Moslems that the True Faith can flourish under Communism. And finally, Hourani's allusion to "those on whom the inherited religion has lost its hold" is an oblique reference to the same features of the prevailing folk religion that I characterized, perhaps too sharply, as decadent and uninspired. Many of the same features, I might add, can also be observed in the folk religion of Western Christian peoples.

After all this has been said, the fact remains that Islam is a living religion, and in terms of both numbers of followers and territorial spread one of the greatest. Moreover, in its doctrine of *jihad* there is a latent source of dynamism—

though now dormant in the folk religion—that is capable of arousal and expression. Whether or not—and how—Islam's fifty million Faithful in the Middle East can be reinspired to defend their faith are questions to which the visiting Westerner finds no answer.

The legal situation in the Middle East is confusing to the Westerner. The confusion is not merely in the mind of the Westerner; it is real. It results from the diversity of the elements from which existing legal systems have been compounded.

Islamic law governs many aspects of life in all the Middle East countries except Turkey, where the legal system has been completely secularized.* Progressively, as political and economic systems have been adapted to the conditions of the contemporary world, traditional Islamic law has tended to be restricted to the regulation of family affairs—marriage, divorce, inheritance, rights of minors, and the like. Correspondingly, Western codes—civil, commercial, and criminal —have been adapted to Middle East concepts and practices, and have been made law by legislative action. This compounding of legal systems, and particularly of the principles upon which they rest, has not been uniform among the countries. No basic principle can be identified as a guide to reconciling the divine origin of Koranic law with the right of men to make their own law.

Westerners are not likely to encounter Islamic law directly in either their personal or business affairs. They are more likely to be concerned with modified Western-type codes

---

* George Lenczowski says in a footnote on p. 424 of his *The Middle East in World Affairs*, Ithaca, N.Y.: Cornell University Press, 2nd ed., 1956: "A major step in this direction [the elimination of undue influence by Islam upon Egypt's public life] was the decree of September 24, 1955, abolishing, as of January 1, 1956, the entire system of Sharia and non-Moslem religious courts." It may still be questioned, however, the extent to which that decree eradicated Islamic law or merely transferred its administration to civil courts.

relevant to their affairs, or with "special laws" negotiated with competent political authorities for particular purposes. The oil-concession agreement is a familiar example. Here a further similarity with the West is found in the fact that, in most cases, the Westerner will deal through lawyers of the country much as he would at home, and will find that if they have not been trained in European law schools, they have at least been trained in European legal principles and procedures. He is likely to find also, however, that even though a given country may have adopted Western codes covering particular matters, the related institutions and principles that make those codes effective in Western countries are deficient or lacking entirely.

The legal systems actually in effect today vary so widely, and are changing so rapidly, that generalizations concerning them are worth little. The starting point common to them all, from which change has taken place, is Islamic law itself. Something like one-fifth of the chapters in the Koran deal with what Westerners would regard as "legal" matters, that is, with secular rather than spiritual guidance, and aimed at "setting limits to man's liberty of action" on earth. Many of those utterances were stated only vaguely, as principles, and to give them statutory interpretation posed problems both during the Prophet's lifetime and afterward. These problems were met by referring to three supplementary sources of illumination which, during the following centuries, came to be accepted by the majority of Moslems as providing authority where the Koran itself was insufficiently explicit.

These three supplementary sources are usually referred to as tradition, analogy, and consensus. Of the three, the one questioned the least was tradition or custom, represented by explanations or practices of the Prophet himself, as reported in statements of reliable informants. The one most useful in

extending an accepted principle to cover new cases was analogy, which rested on logic and reason. Most basic of all, since
the verification of the other two depended upon it, was consensus (among the *ulema,* or learned doctors of religion).
Further, under Islamic law all human conduct can be classified in one of the following five categories: expressly com-
manded, recommended, permitted, disapproved, or absolutely
forbidden.

The broad framework thus sketched in barest outline,
within which Islamic law developed, was subjected to stresses
of two main kinds. The first was doctrinal disputes which
led to schisms within Islam itself, with consequent divergences in the interpretation of the law. Chief among these
was the division between the Sunni (the majority orthodox
party) and the Shia, which started as an essentially political
dispute concerning the succession to the Caliphate. The followers of Ali, son-in-law of the Prophet and the Fourth
Caliph, strove to maintain his line as the sole rightful one;
and the martyrdom of Husain, Ali's son, laid the scene for
the most dramatic schism in the history of Islam. It was during subsequent centuries that the split became doctrinal, as
the Shia repudiated the first three Caliphs—and with them,
of course, the orthodox traditions of law—and introduced a
divergent set of traditions and a wide variety of schismatic
principles.

The second set of stresses arose within the Sunni segment
itself, in the form of disputes, conflicts, and compromises concerning the law. By the fifteenth century the most important
of these divergences had taken fixed forms which still exist
today, mainly in four leading "schools" of orthodox legal
theory. Generally speaking, the four schools recognize one
another's principles as essentially orthodox but alternative
interpretations of the Divine Law.

These doctrinal and legalistic differences within Islam

are significant to a Westerner because they engender a confusing variety of Middle East attitudes toward Western and even toward Islamic legal principles. Thus in countries which are divided between Sunni and Shia, each sect generally has its own system of courts, judges, and procedures, which administer Islamic law in its own fashion, each to its own adherents. When, in addition, Western-type legal codes have been adopted, their administration requires its own system of courts, judges, and procedures as part of the mechanism of government. And the greater the elaboration of the political system, with the adoption of a constitution and law-making bodies, the greater the complexity of the legal organization.

An extreme case of such complexity arises out of British control over the "external affairs" of the Arab coastal shaikhdoms. This control requires a system of courts all its own. British subjects and certain other persons have extraterritorial rights which are adjudicated under British authority. The scope of this authority and the court organization and procedure are set out clearly in a series of Orders in Council, formerly issued by the Government of India but, since the independence of that country, directly by the Government of the United Kingdom. A typical one, applying to Bahrain, opens with the following recital:

Whereas by Treaty, capitulation, grant, usage, sufferance, and other lawful means His Majesty the King has jurisdiction within the territories of the Shaikh of Bahrain. . . . Now, therefore, His Majesty, by virtue and in exercise of the powers in His Majesty vested, is pleased, by and with the advice of his Privy Council, to order, and it is hereby ordered, as follows:

The order goes on to specify the classes of persons subject to it; they include British subjects, other foreigners made subject to it by agreement with the ruling Shaikh (including Americans); and Bahrain subjects employed by them. Disputes involving these Bahrain subjects are dealt with by Joint Courts, whose members are appointed by both the local gov-

ernment and the British. The order also indicates what law
to be applied in certain types of criminal and civil cases, and
makes provision for referring certain types of cases involving
Moslems to a *Qadi* (Moslem judge) for settlement. Certain
other types of cases are referred to special tribunals—for example, disputes between pearling masters and pearl divers to
"the Salifah Court for scrutiny and adjustment."

The introduction of British legal procedure into a traditional Moslem society, despite all the complexities it entails,
has proved over a long period of years to be workable. It has
provided an enduring foundation upon which to build a
legal system sufficiently elastic to an advancing society, while
at the same time preserving the fundamental principles of
Islamic law in matters involving religious doctrine. Also, it
can be said that these British courts, wherever they have been
established, have earned a reputation for impartial justice
that has now become generally accepted among the Arabs—
a tribute seldom paid to their own government-controlled
courts.

The social institutions which have been described briefly
here, that is, the family, tribe, village, and religious and legal
systems, by no means exhaust the list of those encountered
in the Middle East. From the social scientist's point of view,
a very large part of the description of a society must be in
terms of its institutions. To the social scientist, an institution
is any set of cultural or behavioral factors which have become
crystallized into a pattern, so that it tends to produce uniform behavior in a given set of circumstances, and so that it
can be described independently of the persons whose behavior is affected. An institution is thus distinguished from a
set of circumstances that, whatever their importance in a
given case, have not become crystallized in a fixed form.

The observer, especially the policy-maker, has much to

gain by adopting the social scientist's concept of an institution. If he can identify social institutions on their home ground, he will discover (as in the case of Middle East religious and legal systems) that much of the diversity in behavior among groups or regions is not random disorder, but is due only to variations in the detail of an established institution which in other respects may tend to produce uniform behavior. His knowledge of social institutions will also disclose limits within which changes in behavior may be expected to take place with relative ease, that is, without involving change in a basic institution that may be very resistant to change. Most long-established institutions do resist change. On the other hand, increasing numbers of the Middle East peoples, particularly the oncoming generation, are beginning to resist their old institutions.

The observer can see with his own eyes that institutions exist, that they change, and that their changes are intimately related to other changes that are taking place within the society.

Chapter Four

Evidence of Change

IF THE annual reports to Congress on the Mutual Security Act over the last ten years could be taken at face value concerning American achievements through various aid programs, you might conclude that by now there are no "backward countries" left in the world. Nevertheless, according to the report for 1960, the problems that still confront us differ little from those we have always faced.

I do not mean to imply that this is due mainly to bureaucratic incompetence. The same can be said of private consultants and their advisory services to the governments of underdeveloped countries, not excluding some well-meant ones of my own. For example, in Persia since 1911 five major efforts have been made by American advisory staffs, each at the invitation of that government, to create organizations, establish procedures, and train personnel for developmental purposes. Reliable reports in each case tell what was found by the advisers upon arrival, and what was done to put it right. They are singularly the same.*

The most common fault with descriptions of change in underdeveloped countries is that they describe changes in environment—the conditions or circumstances that surround people—rather than change in the people themselves. In many cases the observer not only is unable to describe change in people, but also as a rule he does not even know what aspects of their *behavior* to describe or how to describe them. What he actually sees is only what people are doing at the time of observation, and the circumstances that surround them at that time. He cannot see what people are thinking, or their attitudes and emotions, or their likes and dislikes. Human behavior is influenced by a great number of variables, and these produce their effects at different rates. Many ostensible changes in behavior appear—sometimes spectacularly—on the advancing fringe of a society, and then disappear as factors operating with a greater time lag make their influence felt. If the observer looks only at the advancing fringe he may be misled into believing that the society is changing more rapidly than it is.

One safeguard is to extend the observations over a long enough period to cancel out transient fluctuations in behavior. This still leaves the observer with a wide gap to be bridged before he can be reasonably sure that changes in the people themselves have taken place, or can identify the factors that produced these changes.

Admittedly, to distinguish between change "in people themselves" and change in their observed behavior suggests a vagueness in terms. Nevertheless, from the layman's point of view the distinction seems to be a real one. If in a given set

---

* The five efforts: Morgan Shuster, 1911; Arthur C. Millspaugh, 1922–1927, and again 1943–1945; Overseas Consultants, Inc., 1949–1951; and an advisory group provided by Harvard University under the direction of Professor Edward S. Mason, 1958–1962.

of conditions a person reacts in the same way each time that a certain external stimulus is applied, only his *behavior* is affected in reaction to that stimulus. But if, as time goes on, he begins to react in some other way to that same stimulus, he himself seems to have undergone some internal change. The observer should seek to understand both kinds of change. Why behavior should change in reaction to an external stimulus seems clear enough. But internal change is more obscure. What is it that is changed internally, and what brings such change about?

I can illustrate some aspects of this problem by describing a few of the changes that took place during the first thirty years of American oil-company operations in Bahrain and Saudi Arabia, based for the most part upon direct observation. These were the first oil operations, or indeed modern industries of any kind, in this part of the Arab world. Bahrain, although more advanced in some ways than the other coastal shaikhdoms of the Persian Gulf, was in 1930 still essentially an ancient island community living in its traditional way. Saudi Arabia was practically an unvisited and unknown continent. Therefore these operations started at the very beginning of the impact of Western industrialization.

The American oil men had been told by British friends with many years of experience in other parts of the Middle East that not much could be expected of Arab labor, and that for all but the lowest unskilled grades it would be necessary to import Indians or others for training. The local labor, consisting of peasant villagers, tribesmen, fishermen, pearl divers, and town-fringe indigents, was indeed unskilled. It was also illiterate, impoverished, undernourished, and diseased. These people flocked to the Company for employment, but were seemingly indifferent to wages beyond the few rupees which would provide food for the family group that each supported.

Each payday many workers would quit the job and not be seen again until their wages were spent. Others would take their places, and do the same. Since their wants were simple, not beyond what a few rupees would buy, they were not responsive to inducements to work harder or more regularly, or to learn new skills that would bring more pay. Few of them, in fact, were physically capable of doing more than four hours of work a day at a Western level of effort, so prevalent were disease and malnutrition. Typically, they exhibited no sense of responsibility, or of satisfaction in doing a job well.

Those who were obliged to live in quarters provided by the Company in order to be close to their work preferred *barastis*, built of date-palm leaves, to the cement-block houses put up for them by the Company. They tended to cling together in groups—kinship, village, religious, or other—between which quarrels were frequent. All were distrustful of everyone, particularly of one another. They would not accept paper money, although it was then coming into use by the town merchants, but insisted upon payment in silver rupees— and every coin was "rung" upon cement blocks provided for that purpose outside the pay offices to detect the occasional counterfeit. The spectacle and din of several thousand Arabs ringing rupees on concrete blocks each payday was something not easily forgotten.

As would be expected, there was wide variation in the abilities of these workmen, a variation more baffling than in the West, because the workmen seemed to lack observable traits that would indicate their probable capabilities or aptitudes. For several years the Company's only guide was trial and error. One quality was definitely lacking in them all: a capacity to supervise the work of others. This meant difficulty in training foremen—a highly essential bracket in the hierarchy of industrial administration. These people were not

given to asserting authority over, or accepting it from, one
another unless this authority was based upon their social tradition—although there was almost never any hesitancy about
taking orders from a "European" (British or American) supervisor.

Early experience in getting work done, or training men
for it, brought one surprise after another. The workers lacked
even the most elementary concepts of measurement, tempera-
ture, pressure, or the properties of different materials. One
day in a metal-shop training class I picked up a five-pointed
star that a student had cut from light metal and shaped with
shears and file to duplicate the pattern he was copying. His
own product was neatly done, and his proud smile showed
clearly what he thought of it. But it was not more than three-
quarters as large as the model. Through the interpreter I
asked him why he had not made it like the original, and held
them both up for him to see. He insisted that they were identical, and pointed to a small nick in the model which he had
duplicated faithfully. I put the two pieces behind my back
and then brought out one in each hand, and asked him to
tell me which one he had made. Instantly he picked the
smaller one. I said, "If they are the same, how do you know
which one you made?" He replied to the interpreter, "Tell
the Sahib they are the same—but I am the father of this one,
and know it from all others!"

Their complete lack of knowledge of even the simplest
technical factors frequently prevented them from seeing any
purpose in what they were told to do. The same lack made it
difficult for us to explain. In their own experience there was
seldom any need to explain why a thing was done; it was
done because it had *always* been done. In the early days of
the Bahrain oil company an American supervisor told a work
gang to dig a hole for a telephone pole at a point he had
marked, and indicated that it was to be dug waist deep. He

left on other duties, and returned an hour or two later to find the sand flying, the gang chanting merrily—and a hole twenty feet long, three feet wide, and waist deep, with the pole lying lengthwise along the bottom.

The oil-company operations affected the behavior of these workmen, of course, but the strongest influences stemmed from the communities from which the workmen came. In Bahrain the capital city, Manama, was thirteen miles from the oil fields. Its population of around forty thousand lived mostly in *barastis,* with more pretentious dwellings for the leading merchants built of coral stone laid up with *gutch,* a local plaster of Paris produced by roasting native gypsum rock. Except for the few merchants who prospered from Bahrain's entrepôt trade, importing supplies for transshipment to other Arab centers, local business was centered in the traditional *suq,* or "native bazaar," where the people of Manama and the surrounding communities came for their household needs. Like all Arab bazaars, it contained an astonishing variety of goods, mostly of the cheapest quality available, with no two items alike or any assurance that one bought today could be duplicated tomorrow, or ever, or that spare parts would be available.

Outside the city, the population was clustered in small villages, to which tiny patches of vegetables were attached. In the watered regions of the main island were extensive date gardens, owned by merchants and by the Ruling Family.

By the time the Company had appeared on the scene, the local government, under the guidance of its British Adviser, C. Dalrymple Belgrave (later Sir Charles Belgrave), had already begun to organize a civil service, with Britishers in key posts and well-trained Indians in the rest. Some schools had been established, and a police force supported by a mounted camel corps. At that time these amenities were limited almost exclusively to Manama. In the villages, life went on as before.

Neither the Ruling Family nor the people themselves saw much reason for change, and no reason at all for change that would disturb their traditional way of life.

In Saudi Arabia, in the oil region lying along the Persian Gulf, there were no cities, no British, and no Belgrave. There were only a few scattered villages with scraggly date gardens around the meager water holes. The largest town, Qatif, had a primitive *suq*, and housed the local government officials. Qatif and the neighboring village of Dhahran grew rapidly after the Company moved in, largely through migrations from other parts of Saudi Arabia, but with increasing numbers of immigrants from surrounding Arab countries.

The labor situation and general social conditions facing the Company were much the same in Saudi Arabia as in Bahrain. But in many other ways the two cases were not closely comparable. Thus, in Saudi Arabia the Company had direct relations with the government without British intercession, and this had both advantages and disadvantages. The Saudi government permitted no British employees. In Bahrain the Company was required as a condition of the concession (a condition stipulated by the British) to use British employees as far as possible, and to conduct all dealings with the local government through a British representative. An Arab who had worked in both countries was once asked to compare his American and British bosses and say which he liked better. "The British," he replied promptly. "The British Sahib will say, 'Boy! Fetch me that spanner!' I get the spanner and take it to him. But the American Sahib says, 'Boy! Fetch me that spanner!' and before I can get it he jumps up and gets it himself. Then my friends laugh at me!"

During the next ten years, say until about 1940, some remarkable changes took place. In Bahrain (which had a start of around five years over the corresponding work in Saudi Arabia), a casual observer might walk the length of the oil refinery and scarcely see a European. They were there, of course, in the offices, control rooms, laboratories, and shops. But the Arabs were everywhere, not only as "coolie" labor, but in maintenance squads working under their own foremen, and also as mechanics' helpers, truck and tractor drivers, hoist operators, pumpers, gaugers, carpenters, painters, pipefitters, and even acetylene welders. In the oil fields they were performing semiskilled work on the floor of a rotary drilling rig—under the watchful eye of an American driller or "tool pusher"—and high overhead in the derrick. In the laboratories they were conducting routine tests for the control of processes. In the shops they operated machine tools and rewound motors and transformers. Even in the offices, where, in Bahrain, most of the skilled clerks were Indians, young Arabs were sorting material and time slips and using adding machines.

By that time nearly all of the workers were able to last for a full shift, and most of them a double shift if necessary—a consequence of good food and freedom from endemic diseases. Training classes were crowded. Off-shift they were playing soccer or cricket (in Saudi Arabia, baseball), or watching matches between rival departments. Also, they were complaining about housing inadequacies, or about a few flies buzzing noisily in a bunkhouse—even though in their own villages flies were so thick they had to be brushed off with one hand while food was put into the mouth with the other.

Many changes ran even deeper. After ten years there was a stable nucleus of a labor force, regular in attendance, and—grading upward according to individual characteristics—intent upon learning new jobs and advancing into those with increased responsibilities and higher pay.

There were limits, of course, to how fast such advancement could take place and how far it could go in ten years. Men who were mature when they started with the Company were practically all illiterate, and as long as they could not read orders or make necessary records, certain jobs for which they might have qualified in other ways were closed to them. Boys who knew that they must attend school if they wished to work for the Company still met the traditional resistance of their elders in the villages who, for various reasons, thought schooling less important than tending sheep or catching bait. Also, health programs were one thing within the Company precincts and quite another in the unsanitary villages where most of the workers went home to sleep.

Thus many new ideas that began to permeate the thinking of those who worked for the Company came into conflict with the traditional ideas of the family, village, or larger community of which they were also members. Such conflict had to be reduced before a change in traditional ways could be made without the risk of general disapproval which few employees were willing to accept. As an illustration, an Arab teacher with much experience in rural areas once told me that a school intended to serve several villages could build up its attendance much faster if it concentrated on one village at a time. The reason was that if only a few boys from each village came, they would be jeered at by their fellows at home for going to school instead of taking their traditional part in village life. But if the school were opened to only one village to begin with, and enrolled enough boys to establish going to school as the thing to do, nearly all the boys of that village would attend. Adding successive villages would work the same way. In no case would the boys actually attending school be outnumbered at home by those who did not. The same effect would be felt by their parents.

Another example was the resistance met by the Company in its efforts to persuade employees that trousers or coveralls were much safer around refinery operations or construction jobs than their traditional outer garment, the *thoub,* which resembled a Western nightgown. The *thoub* was forever being caught on some projecting part—or worse yet, in moving machinery. If a workman were rebuked or ridiculed in his own village for adopting European dress, even the sight of a fellow worker being snapped up by a steel cable and wrapped around a rapidly revolving hoist drum under a dozen coils of wire rope before the machine could be stopped would not persuade him to change his costume—although it might make him *want* to change.

The Company found, as might be expected, that younger age groups learned more quickly than older ones and were less bound by traditional practices, also that any group relatively isolated from its home surroundings was more adaptable to new practices than groups living in their own villages. More obscure differentiations were also disclosed by experience. In Saudi Arabia, for example, it became accepted as a generalization that tribesmen from the hinterland excelled villagers as truck and tractor drivers, watchmen, or operators on jobs that required individual resourcefulness and dependability. Villagers, on the other hand, usually were better than tribesmen on work that required "gang" performance.

From a broader viewpoint, the changes that took place within the society itself during the ten-year period from 1930 to 1940 were equally striking, although different from those affecting the Company directly. In Bahrain the effects of Company operations cannot be separated from Belgrave's achievements in government administration. Both contributed to the introduction of new ideas, capabilities, and institutions, and to opportunities for new satisfactions. Under the stimulus of increased purchasing power, merchants filled their shelves with new types of goods which were eagerly sought by consumers. As the businessmen's capital increased, some of them started bus lines to transport workmen to their jobs, and others equipped themselves with trucks for contract hauling, or became small building contractors.

In the communities as in the Company, there were limitations both as to the kind of change that was readily accepted and as to the rate at which it took place. New ways of doing *new* things were accepted more readily than new ways of doing *old* things. Thus the owner of a food shop would buy an electric refrigerator to chill Pepsi-Cola, because if served warm it would come out as foam, but his meat and fish would continue to hang on a string in the open, exposed to sun, flies, and dust. New types of tools would be used for new types of work (as in oil-company operations), and reasonable skill in their use would be eagerly acquired. But traditional types of work, such as carpentry, masonry, or boatbuilding, continued to be done in the old way.

Thus, although Bahrain has been known since antiquity for its boatbuilding, its boats did not meet the exacting requirements of the Company. The reason was, in part, that joints in frames and planking were poorly made and fastened, by Company standards. To remedy this, modern tools and fastenings were necessary. The Company had no great difficulty in having boats that met its requirements built in its own shops by local workmen; but for local boatyards to turn out their products in this way would have meant the end of an ancient guild of boatbuilders.

This case is not as simple as it may seem. What may appear to be a single tradition, which could be changed by merely demonstrating the superiority of a new way, usually involves an entire pattern of traditional ways. I once had a sailboat built in a local boatyard for our own use at Umm A'Sabaan Island. I watched the process almost daily for several months. The gray-bearded builders spent some time each day sitting about and puffing in turn on the common *nargilah* (water pipe), arguing over the warp of each plank as it went into the hull, the suitability of available knee braces and ribs, and the placement of the mast. Other master builders dropped by each day from other yards to sip cardamum-incensed coffee and to criticize the decisions that had been reached. Many specially shaped pieces had been bought initially while still parts of a living tree, and perhaps even allowed to grow to a certain size before cutting and curing for use. All the builders knew what knee braces, ribs, and spars each one had in his stock, and pieces were occasionally traded after drawn-out bargaining in which all present took part.

A boat put together from a blueprint, its parts cut to a pattern with modern tools and fastened with factory bolts, bypasses all such ritual. The completed craft may be better at withstanding a storm. But what happens to the skill, the pride, and the prestige of the master boatbuilder, and the joy he takes in his work? And why should he believe that the modern-built boat is superior to those used for thousands of years by his people?

Still other examples support the observation that innovation itself does not necessarily meet resistance but that resistance is met when a traditional practice is faced with change. When airplanes first began to visit the Middle East countries, even the nomadic tribesmen were eager to ride in them. The same can be said of bicycles and automobiles when they first appeared. But nothing could persuade them to change the design of their camel saddles, though almost any change in those, from a Westerner's viewpoint, would have been an improvement. On our own island our boatmen vied with one another for a place in our small speedboat, powered with an outboard motor, which made the crossing to Budaiya in one fifth the time it would take to sail in our Arab *banoosh*. But when we fitted lee-boards to the *banoosh* that reduced leeway in a cross-wind and enabled us to fetch Budaiya jetty in one reach, they muttered deep disapproval and used them only when we were aboard. Clearly, lee-boards were not a proper part of a *banoosh*, and the boatmen preferred to drift half a mile down wind and laboriously pole the boat back up to the landing rather than change their way of sailing.

During the first ten years of oil operations in Bahrain, relatively few changes in traditional practices were made (and still fewer in Saudi Arabia) except within the Company precincts where Company rules were enforced. Most of the observable changes were innovations that did not conflict directly with traditions, or require that a choice be made between the old way and the new. Thus, although merchants and businessmen expanded their activities, their methods of doing business showed little change—and the traditional methods of the Arab bazaar are not well suited to modern enterprise.

It was not until the third decade, starting in 1950, that deep-seated changes in the underlying character of the society became conspicuous, both in Bahrain and in Saudi Arabia. In the sphere of oil activities, an increasing number of employees began to retire on pension after twenty years or more of continuous service. Each of those pensioners became a source of new attitudes and influences among the oncoming generations. Within the Company organization itself there were Arab foremen and skilled artisans in nearly all trades, and in the refineries and drilling operations equally skilled men performing specialized work with high competence. Much of the construction and maintenance work, moreover, was being done by Arab contractors with their own organizations and equipment.

It is worth noting that the spectacular growth in contract work and in Company purchases made through local merchants did not take place solely because new skills and markets had been developed, though both were necessary to that growth. A more basic change was in the Arabs' concept of the meaning of a contract. They came to understand that a contract entails faithful performance—quality of work, time, adherence to specifications, agreed cost—and that such performance requires responsible and continuous attention. To importers and suppliers the contract meant that stocks must be maintained at agreed-upon levels, and that quality must be as specified. To both suppliers and contractors it meant that modern methods of management must be adopted, including planning and scheduling, accounting, inspection and testing, and fair practices toward their own employees to avoid interruptions in their services. Both learned, too, that a contract, under the conditions just stated, was a capital asset, and could be placed with a bank as security for operating funds or for paying invoices for imported materials.

In the community at large, some changes were more marked in Bahrain than in Saudi Arabia, partly because of Bahrain's head start but mainly because of Belgrave's contributions to government administration. As for changes that met the eye, Manama in the 1950's was no longer a sprawling town of muddy alleys and a clutter of palm-leaf *barastis*, but a modernized city with paved streets, a modern power plant, piped water, and a steadily expanding residential section that would do credit to many a Western city. The *suq* kept its place to serve the traditional needs of the population, but their newer needs were served by a modern shopping district where merchants displayed in their show windows about the same brands of wearing apparel, tinned foods, pharmaceutical supplies, household furnishings, kitchen utensils, hardware, machinery, radios, and automobile spare parts that would be found in a city of the same size in Europe or the United States. The obvious prosperity of the merchants was evidence that there were consumers for those goods.

An annual agricultural exhibition, at which villagers competed for prizes handed out by the Ruler, reflected the work of the Bahrain Government Experimental Agricultural Station. Large modern hospitals, supplemented by rural clinics and a capable public health organization, provided free medical care for the people. A labor law regulated the terms of employment to protect workers against exploitation or abuse.

Most important of all the directly observable changes were the schools, primary and secondary, mainly in the city but scattered through the village areas as well. The schools were crowded with healthy-looking youngsters, nearly all in simple uniform—shorts and short-sleeved shirts—studying about the same subjects in the classrooms and playing the same games on the playgrounds that might be observed in a Western country, with allowances for national differences. The crowning achievement in this field was not the modern school buildings or the vocational training classes; it was the school for girls, the first in this part of the Arab world except for small classes conducted by American missionaries. The girls' school had been started with infinite tact by Belgrave and his wife many years before, and had risen to become a source of influence difficult to measure.

There are few contrasts in the Middle East more striking than between the traditional Moslem women of the poorer class (at least as they appear to the Western observer) and modern girl students. The women were like scarecrows, faces masked and figures hidden beneath shapeless black garments. For the most part they were kept behind closed doors except when chattering around the public well or scuttering out of sight at the approach of a stranger. By report, they were frequently diseased, and generally treated like farm animals. The modern girl student wears an attractive Western frock until, at marriageable age, she leaves school to take her place in the adult life of the community.

In Bahrain, experience showed that girls, on the average, not only were better students than boys, but also continued their studies until they became marriageable, whereas a large number of boys dropped out to start work. These girls, moreover, are much sought after by the better-educated young men, and after marriage exercise a strong influence over their husbands, particularly in planning the children's futures. Polygamy is distinctly a thing of the past, as far as these young people are concerned. Each year has brought increasing pressure for complete emancipation of women in Bahrain in the same way that it has taken place, at least in all but remote provinces, in Turkey, Persia, and some other countries. As a traditional institution, *purdah* (concealment of women) is still the practice in Bahrain, and even more strictly so in Saudi Arabia, but is meeting more and more resistance among the oncoming generation. Its diminution is both a cause and a result of the weakening of traditional life among the Arabs.

Some indication of the changes that have taken place in people, as distinguished from transient changes in behavior, can be seen in the composition of the Arabian American Oil Company work force in Saudi Arabia, according to a recently published report by that company.* A completely raw, untrained Arab force began work in the middle 1930's. By 1950 there were more than two thousand Arab employees rated—by the rigorous standards of a highly technological industry—as "semiskilled or higher." By 1960 this number had increased to around nine thousand, in a total force that had remained approximately constant in size. At the opening of the 1950's none of the Arabs had qualified as "senior staff," but forty-four were thus classified in 1960, working at the same level as European and American university graduates.

The significance of the change goes beyond these figures. Considerable numbers of Arabs had left the Company to enter government service or to start private businesses of their own.

---

* *Aramco Handbook,* prepared by Roy Lebkicher, George Rentz, and Max Steineke, New York, 1960, p. 211.

Moreover the figures, striking as they are, represent only a fraction of the total number whose capabilities had been increased but who were not yet qualified for these higher classifications. On the other hand, one must not lose sight of the fact that the total number of Saudi Arabians thus far directly affected by the Company's training programs, including the employees' families, would not exceed a few hundred thousand out of a total population of six or seven million. Moreover, it must not be overlooked that even in Saudi Arabia (and also in Bahrain), where conditions were especially favorable for accelerated change, it took a full generation to bring about these changes.

Generally similar changes have been taking place in other parts of the Middle East where corresponding opportunities have been provided. An outstanding example of the way in which change in people—in their ideas and attitudes—can be used as a means of producing changes in their surrounding environment is the work of the Near East Foundation, an American philanthropic institution with headquarters in New York. One of its most notable successes has been in the very country, Persia, which has shown the greatest resistance to social reforms. A basic principle of this Foundation's work has been the belief that if people can first be made to desire a change in their conditions of life, it becomes relatively simple to enable them to make progressive steps toward that change. This is the reverse of the process ordinarily employed by many planners of development and "aid" programs, who first decide what the people *ought* to want, and then set about producing those changed conditions in the hope that the people will want them.

The limited resources that have been available to the Near East Foundation have obliged its leaders to follow a course that makes the most of the people's own resources, with only a minimum use of capital and imported technical aid.

The fact that they concentrate on changing the people, however, rather than on changes in physical conditions, has enabled them to hold the gains they make, and to use them as "seed" for more extended change. Although progress by this method is slow to begin with, and rarely spectacular, its results increase in geometric ratio as its circle of influence widens. Moreover, the Near East Foundation's experience has shown that results produced within one such widening circle will be picked up and duplicated elsewhere, where progress will be even more rapid because many of the initial problems met in developing confidence and introducing change will not be faced again.

A recent report of the Foundation includes the following brief statement concerning its methods.*

The Near East Foundation, by invitation of the host government, begins its work in each country by operating a demonstration in a rural area. It creates an "Island of Progress" which the government can absorb and duplicate on a national basis. It demonstrates improved methods within the capacity of the people to adapt them into their pattern of rural development. It believes that trained manpower is the greatest contribution it can make to any country and sets up training institutions for the sub-professional skills where there is greatest shortage. It believes in the dignity of labor and teaches that manual labor is not incompatible with educated people.

The Near East Foundation conducts its activities in close cooperation with the host government and desires to turn over its activities and operations as soon as these activities can be successfully administered by the host government.

With these policies in view, the Near East Foundation started operations in 1946 in the Varamin Plains (approximately twenty-five miles southwest of Teheran). The original demonstration area consisted of five villages, belonging to an orphanage, and was centered around the village of Mamazon. The activities gradually grew until the program reached the three hundred and sixty villages of the Varamin Plains, and now [in 1960] has become the full responsibility of the cooperating Ministries. . . .

* Near East Foundation, New York, Annual Report for 1960.

The areas of demonstration and improvement had modest beginnings. During the initial stages of the program, confidence and acceptance of the program by the rural people was needed. Slowly and gradually the program involved the daily lives of most all the rural people throughout the Varamin Plains. . . . The program included advancement in agriculture, education, home and family welfare, sanitation, and community development.

Persia, too, was the scene of an episode showing how a simple and helpful innovation can make headway among peasants but be blocked at higher levels. In 1949 the engineers of the Seven-Year Plan tried to introduce a small oil stove into Persian villages. Its purpose was to provide a low-cost source of heat for all household purposes. In Persia's rugged winters this was a dire need, met only in part by the traditional charcoal brazier or—if the peasant could not afford charcoal—by burning dried cow dung that would otherwise have been used as fertilizer. In a typical village these pats of dung would cover the sides of peasant houses for drying during the summer, and would then be piled on the roof for use in the winter. A rough estimate indicated that thousands of tons of valuable fertilizer were burned each year, also that unless the devastation of forests by charcoal burners could be stopped, the few forest areas left in the country, so important for water conservation, would soon disappear. Nevertheless, heat was essential, and there was no other fuel. By the first snowfall the land would be stripped clean of brushwood, weeds, and even dried grass for miles around a village—an important cause of land erosion by wind and rain.

Persia was one of the leading oil-producing countries of the world, but no way had ever been provided to make it available as fuel for Persia's forty-five or fifty thousand villages. The Plan engineers suggested that a simple stove and a cheap grade of kerosene, widely used over the country, would solve several problems at once. Government officials were indifferent. The Anglo Iranian Oil Company, already in a deadlock with the government over concessional disputes, resisted the whole idea.

The engineers persisted, and learned through the Shell Oil Company management in London that a cheap and generally suitable stove had already been developed and used successfully in some of the European countries during the war. Details were obtained, and after some months of preliminary work several hundred small stoves were produced in one of the munition factories that Reza Shah had built to make rifles for the army. The stove was of such design, moreover, that it could be made even by semiskilled metal workers in any bazaar. The factory cost was about one dollar per stove; the bazaar cost was a few hours of labor and some scrap metal.

Winter was just coming on when this lot of heaters was put out for test in a series of villages representing as wide a range of conditions as could be found. To be included, a village had to agree to certain terms: everyone must use the "Plan" stove and nothing else for all cooking and heating; they must follow instructions closely, permit periodic inspections, keep track of the amount of oil used, not sell the oil to other villages, and so on. In return they would get, free of charge, the stoves and all the fuel required for the entire winter. Most of the villages approached agreed to take part in the test. A capable young Persian engineer, trained at the University of California, was in charge of the project, and stayed with it night and day. In a jeep, over almost roadless country and in every kind of weather, he visited one village after another, modifying the equipment, trimming wicks, adapting utensils and cooking methods to a new kind of heat, soothing exasperated housewives, dressing burned fingers, and recovering stolen kerosene. Despite all difficulties the test went on. As the cold winter set in, a simple oven was added to improve the stove for space heating. At times a village would revolt, but the reason would be discovered and corrected. Perhaps better ventilation was needed. Uneven floors required a switch from four legs to three, to keep the stove steady. Once, toward spring, in a single week every village discarded the stove and returned to the traditional cooking methods, with neither complaint nor explanation. The reason: it was cheese-making time, and the large flat pans that held the milk were too big for the stove to support. The peasants accepted this as a manifestation of fate, but within a few days a large ring with its own supports was produced and distributed by the factory, and the cheese-makers were happy again. All the villagers' problems seemed finally to have been solved, and other villages were clamoring for the "Plan" stove.

Other problems arose, however, this time with officials who were asked to appropriate the moderate funds to expand the scale of the operation; with greedy merchants who sought to get in on the deal through which cheap kerosene would become available; with the oil company, which objected to an upset of its price structure; and with some Plan officials who were more interested in letting multimillion-dollar contracts for new factories and power plants than in providing heat for millions of simple peasants and conserving valuable resources as a byproduct. The same preferences were shown by the American aid team that was in Persia at that time.

The story ends where it started—with cow dung drying on the walls of huts in the summer to supplement twigs and charcoal as fuel for the winter. The evidence of one winter's trial showed that the peasants were ready to change their ways of a thousand years, with benefit to themselves and to the country. But when this change required change at higher decision-making levels, resistance became too strong.

There are something like seventy-five million people in the Middle East countries, and three quarters of them have scarcely yet begun to change in ways that can be described in familiar technical or economic terms. Still, that they are changing is vividly apparent. The difficulty is in knowing precisely *what* to describe. Among the innumerable things that we observe—physical environment, behavior, events— which things are significant to our better understanding of the Middle East and its ways?

Chapter Five

Bahrain: The Anatomy of Change

"IT WAS 1954, a year of continual political unrest, strikes, demonstrations, and disturbances starting with sectarian quarrels which gave place to agitation directed against the Government. Bahrain had become a very different place to what it was when I had first known it." So writes Sir Charles Belgrave in his memoirs covering thirty years as Adviser to the Shaikh of Bahrain.* Belgrave goes on to describe and explain events that marked the stages of increasing unrest and demonstrations against the Bahrain Government which culminated in 1957 when British troops had to restore order.

In comparison with other national rebellions Bahrain's was only a tempest in a test-tube, but for that very reason it may be a good one to examine more carefully. For what was taking place in Bahrain during those eventful years of rebellion was closely paralleled by generally similar events in nearly every other country in the Middle East and many others outside it. Bahrain, that is, appeared to be following a

---

* Sir Charles Belgrave, *Personal Column*. London: Hutchinson & Co., 1960, pp. 199 ff.

pattern.

This little country, consisting of a small group of islands in the Persian Gulf a few miles off the Arabian coast, with a population in 1960 of around 145,000, has an archeological history extending back to the fourth millennium before the Christian era. For the last three-quarters of a century it has lain under the rule of the Al Khalifah family, with British treaty protection. Until around 1930, life there differed little from that in other semi-dormant Arab communities. The population, like that of most coastal Arab communities, is an ethnic mixture, with an upper class of relatively pure Arab lineage and the rest an indeterminate blend of presumably indigenous stock with admixtures down through the ages reflecting, in the way of such things, countless visits of sea-faring folk and invasions from other shores. There is also an important remnant of earlier Persian rule in a segment of Arab-Persian stock, and an Indian community with its own distinctive characteristics. The prevailing religion is Moslem, divided between Sunni and Shia. The Indians are largely Roman Catholic, though some are Hindu and Moslem.

To this very brief sketch must be added a word about the role of the British, which is an important factor in the case. Since the birth of the East India Company in 1600, the Middle East has lain across the British "life line" connecting the homeland with its eastern colonies. The Persian Gulf was bordered by barbaric peoples, and to make both land and sea routes secure the British took steps to control the coastal chiefs, using their sea power to suppress piracy and later the slave trade. Over the years British relations with local shaikhs developed into formal treaties which had the effect of protecting friendly rulers against both internal and external threats, in return for which they granted to the British complete authority over their relations with other countries. In this way Britain accomplished her dual purpose of rendering her commercial routes safe and closing the area to other European powers that sought strategic footholds there.

In principle British authority did not extend to the internal affairs of these Shaikhdoms, but in practice the maintenance of law and order has required the frequent exercise of force, even to the present time. British political authority was represented by political officers stationed at key points, Bahrain among them. Over them all was the Political Resident, formerly stationed in Bushire on the Persian shore but transferred to Bahrain after the outbreak of World War II. Persian Gulf affairs were administered routinely by the Government of India until the independence of that country and thereafter directly by the British Foreign Office. Friendly shaikhs dependent upon the British for their tenure as rulers were normally acquiescent to British demands, but many others remained intractable, and the tribal populations quite generally resented British intrusion into their traditional ways of life.

Bahrain's modern awakening, like that of most Arab countries, dates from the close of the First World War, although the main events that changed the long course of its history occurred in the decade of the 1930's. The principal ones were the engagement of Belgrave as Adviser to the Ruler, the discovery of oil by an American company, and a worldwide wave of awakening influences spread largely by radio, cinema, and increasing travel, bringing a stream of new ideas, hopes, and aspirations to the people of Bahrain as to those of many other underdeveloped countries.

During this decade and continuing after it, there were vast changes in the economic and social life of the country. Most conspicuous was the rebuilding of Manama, the capital and principal city, but even more significant was the manifest trend toward throwing off traditional ways and adopting Western ways instead. But many traditions held, or gave way only slowly. The Arab elite, and particularly the continually ramifying Ruling Family, clung stubbornly to traditional privileges. Isolated communities, and quite generally the elder generation, changed few of their ways. Islam in its spiritual aspects resisted all heretical intrusions, even though its secular code adjusted to the necessities and conveniences of Western innovations.

By 1954 new pressures from various sources broke through the old restraints. The first outbreaks of violence took the form, as Belgrave has stated, of sectarian quarrels. A trivial dispute between children over a bicycle grew into a serious conflict between Sunni and Shia villages, with two deaths in its wake. This conflict spread, only to unite both sects against the Ruler's courts and magistrates on the grounds of incompetence and corruption, both indictments having some basis in fact. Once traditional authority had been challenged openly, additional reasons for revolt were put forward, not all of equal merit but all inflammatory in the mouths of rabble-rousers. These were followed by additional outbursts of violence. Deaths occurred when police fired into mobs. Skillfully organized general strikes paralyzed the local economy and defied all local authority.

There was enough substance to some of the popular complaints to win the restrained support of British political officials, and for a time it looked as though the time-honored formula of "divide and rule" might be applied locally to keep the situation in check by partial support of both sides. But elsewhere in the Middle East, particularly in Egypt, Jordan, and Iraq, anti-British feelings were rising. Part, at least, of the rebel leadership in Bahrain was strongly influenced by the rebel leaders in these other countries, and the people themselves were not immune to widespread propaganda from these sources. When the showdown came toward the end of 1957 it was no longer a "sectarian quarrel" but a well-organized revolt of the people—not against their Ruler personally or against Belgrave as his adviser or against the British individuals they knew—but against the whole historic process of which these were the symbols and which had denied them what the modern world had granted to others.

The more fortunate or more alert segments of the population had profited by exploiting new opportunities, but only to become more aware than ever of still greater opportunities blocked by a self-centered and reactionary government maintained in power by the British. One segment was a growing middle class of prospering businessmen who paid lip-service to the Ruling Family but secretly supported the rebels, partly on principle and partly through fear of reprisals by uncontrolled mobs. There was an even larger segment that had not benefited directly from increased economic activity and relatively little from the new schools, hospitals, and other social reforms that as yet reached only limited groups. This segment, mainly the inhabitants of town fringes and outlying villages, became more aware than ever of what seemed to be discriminations against them and responded blindly to popular leaders who urged them to revolt.

The climax came when the British, by now a definite target of the rebellion, moved troops to Bahrain in 1957 and supported the Ruler in restoring order. But banishing the top leaders to Saint Helena and jailing the lesser ones locally did not put an end to the conflict. It merely put a lid on the kettle.

Clearly, what happened in Bahrain—as in other cases of rebellion in the Middle East—was brought about by the interaction of many factors, cultural, social, political, and economic, all acting in various combinations. But as a point of attack in our understanding of the rebellion, we can take the set of factors associated with nationalism. In recent years many outbreaks of rebelliousness and violence in the Middle

East have been attributed by Western observers to increasing nationalism, although those who use the term do not always make clear precisely what they mean by it. Nationalism of some kind can be manifested in many ways—chauvinism, xenophobia, conquest. But if we define nationalism here as "the assertion by a people of its claim to a distinctive national identity entitling it to live its own life in its own fashion," * we have a definition with a good cutting edge for our purposes.

What was the origin of nationalism in Bahrain, how did it spread within the society, and how did it affect the exercise and acceptability of authority over the affairs of the society?

One factor that clearly influenced the growth of nationalism was the acceptance of the principle of *self-determination;* that is, that every person has the right of self-determination in matters that concern himself, so long as the exercise of this right does not infringe upon the similar right of other persons. From this principle it follows that any group of persons, —family, tribe, or village—that reaches a consensus concerning such rights can apply the same principle to the group as a whole. Extending the principle, various groups that reach a consensus concerning rights that are common among them can form successively larger groups. Thus if these rights concerned religious worship the collectivity would comprise a faith, like Christianity or Islam, within which progressively smaller groups would be allowed to adopt rules of their own as long as these remained compatible with the enveloping consensus. If these rights concerned political authority, the

---

* This definition was supplied by Rupert Emerson, Professor of Government at Harvard University, in his contribution to *Ideology and Foreign Affairs,* a study prepared by the Harvard Center for International Affairs at the request of the Senate Committee on Foreign Relations. (See Committee Print No. 10, S. Res. 336, 85th Congress, and S. Res. 31, 86th Congress, U.S. Government Printing Office, Washington, Jan. 17, 1960, p. 10.) For a more comprehensive treatment of nationalism by the same author, see his *From Empire to Nation.* Cambridge: Harvard University Press, 1960.

largest collectivity within which consensus was reached would comprise a nation, which would reject external political authority as not arising from that consensus, but would allow lesser internal groups their own rights of self-determination subject to the unifying consensus.

However, in a society which traditionally has looked upon various servitudes imposed by others as being in the natural order of things, it is not likely that all members would accept such a right simultaneously, as a sudden release from long established restraints, or as a new right. In Bahrain the concept of self-determination worked its way through most of the population at a varying rate. Early in the period of unrest there was little evidence of any concepts except those long fixed by tradition; by 1957 the popular battlecry was "Bahrain for the Bahrain people!" What we must do now is identify groups which accepted the principle of self-determination and progressively combined in its support until it became a dominant unifying idea among the people. And as we do this we must seek also to identify the main factors which seemed to accelerate or retard the spread of this idea.

Here we can profit from the work of Karl Deutsch, a social scientist who made a rather elaborate analysis of the way in which a new unifying idea spreads through a traditional society.* Although the information we have about Bahrain does not permit a rigorous application of Deutsch's analysis, we can use his findings as a lead to understanding what happened there. In very brief summary, Deutsch's study leads to the following general conclusions relevant to Bahrain. In a traditional society the spread of a new way of thinking, for example an ideological concept such as nationalism, Communism, or democracy, or the acceptance of new social relationships or of a new language, is dependently related to the

---

* Karl Deutsch, *Nationalism and Social Communication.* New York: M.I.T. and John Wiley & Sons, 1953.

communication system through which ideas, or "messages," are introduced, exchanged, and disseminated among the people. When the communication system—the ways and means through which ideas are exchanged—reaches a certain general level of effectiveness (here we can disregard transitional stages), the society becomes mobilized for social action. Mobilization is a state or condition affecting a society or a given segment of it, which makes it possible for a new idea to stimulate a nearly simultaneous response throughout the society. Before a society becomes mobilized, the introduction of a new idea may stimulate individual action—even in many individuals—but inadequate communication among them inhibits social action by the people as a whole.

When a given idea is introduced into a mobilized population the responses it stimulates, though widespread, are not necessarily identical throughout the society; the idea may be accepted by some and rejected by others. In respect to this new way of thinking, therefore, new groups may be formed. In Deutsch's terminology the part of the total population which accepts the new way of thinking is the *assimilated* group. In all, he recognizes nine possible groupings of the population. What he finds significant is the changing ratios between these groups as shifts in their numbers take place over a span of time.

For our present purposes we can focus upon two groups. The first is the mobilized group, which is the part of the total population that has become mobilized for social action. The second is the assimilated group, that part which has accepted the new idea as a guide for social action. Deutsch further identifies the mobilized group as follows:

Within any geographical setting and any population, economic, social and technological developments mobilize individuals for relatively more intensive communication. We may call this the social and political public, or the *mobilized population,* and we may delimit this mobilized population (i.e., population mobilized for mass communication) by various yardsticks of measurement: the set of persons who live in towns; the set of persons engaged in occupations other than agriculture, forestry and fishing; the set of persons who read a newspaper at least once a week; the set of persons who pay direct taxes to a central government; or who are directly subject to military conscription; the set of persons who have attended public or private schools for at least four years; the set of persons attending markets at least once a month; the set of persons sending or receiving a letter at least once a month; the set of literate adults, of movie-goers, or radio listeners, of registered voters for elections, or of insured persons under social security schemes; or all persons working for money wages in units with five or more employees; and many more.*

In any particular case it is possible to add to these criteria to take local circumstances into account. In Bahrain, for example, we might add the set of persons who have ready access to scheduled bus services, or those who regularly participate in organized competitive sports. The sets of persons indicated by all these criteria overlap, of course, but common to all of them is some circumstance that facilitates the communication and spread of an idea—any idea that may be introduced.

In 1930, the part of Bahrain's population mobilized for mass communication was small indeed, by whatever criteria we use. This group was limited to a very few relatively prosperous trading families in Manama whose business activities brought them in touch with the outside world, and a small number of other persons whose work with shipping, association with American missionaries, or the like, met the minimum criteria of mobilization as Deutsch defined it.†

The unmobilized group in 1930 thus included nearly the entire population. Roughly half the people of the country lived in Manama or its sister-city Muharraq (separated by a

---

* Deutsch, *op. cit.*, p. 102.

† Although most of the detail that follows is based upon my own observations and notes, the Annual Report of the Government of Bahrain prepared by Sir Charles Belgrave is a compendium of information, descriptive and statistical, for the three decades 1930–1960.

narrow waterway), the other half in villages scattered over the northern portion of the main island, where water supplies were available, and in fishing villages along the shore. Physical facilities for communication were almost entirely lacking, both within and between communities and between the people and the world outside. Radios and cinema had not yet been introduced. Schooling for the masses was limited to elementary religious instruction that did not have literacy as an aim. The Koran was memorized by rings of children squatting around a *mullah* and chanting the holy words. Except for primitive agriculture and fishing (which are not included in the criteria of mobilization) and primitive bazaar occupations, there were almost no economic activities for the masses. The few families that were engaged in entrepôt trade provided only stevedoring and menial employment for others. In the arid part of the main island there was a small drifting segment of Bedouin Arabs with their goats and camels, traditionally attached to the Ruling Shaikh and serving as a nostalgic reminder of his own family's ancient tribal lineage.

In 1930, the Ruling Family itself would have passed none of the tests for mobilization, at least not in a meaningful manner. The Shaikhs of Bahrain lived in the way of their past, a dignified and gracious way by their own standards and even by some of ours, and with deep convictions as to what that way should be. But what went on in the outside world, or even within their own, so long as it remained undisturbed, concerned them little.

In addition to the fixed population there was in Bahrain, as in all seaport communities, a transient or semitransient population that came and went according to their various purposes. Many of the Indians were of this class—merchants, traders, or artisans who lived in Bahrain for a time and were supplanted by others. There were also transient Arabs from other coastal and inland communities. At any given time the transients might represent a substantial group in Manama, but their permanent interests were not in Bahrain, and the composition of the group itself underwent continuous change.

This, then, was the unmobilized population in Bahrain in 1930, insensitive to modern ideas and unequipped for communication among themselves.

Now we must see how the total population was divided on the basis of *assimilation* to new ideas and concepts, and in particular to the principle of self-determination. It is difficult, however, to delimit the part of the total population that had a deep awareness of its right to self-determination, as distinguished from an ordained destiny of servitude to others or to traditional ways. For the moment, let us leave the defining characteristics unprecise, just as the concept of self-determination was unprecise in the minds of the people themselves. Later, with the growth of popular awareness that social and political servitudes might be either borne or thrown off, the groups that chose to throw them off did this in ways that made them distinguishable and identification more sure.

There is much evidence to show that, with certain reservations, the principle of self-determination is deeply embedded in the Arab culture and in the Moslem faith. Although the principle is obscured by traditional class distinctions and certain cultural patterns which take precedence over it, self-determination as a basic right of the individual and of the social group shows up clearly in the institutions described earlier—family, village, tribal, religious, and legal. For example, the *hadith* (traditions of the Prophet) establish as a principle of divine law that God will forgive a repentant for an act which has affected the repentant alone, but if the rights of another have been transgressed, forgiveness by the injured one must come first. This injunction provides a basis for the qualified right of self-determination. But at a traditional level of social organization it is not always possible to say, on the basis of observed evidence alone, whether any given conduct explicitly manifests the assertion of a right, or merely conforms with a tradition to which there is no accepted alternative.

During this early period in Bahrain most of the rights of decision did not rest in the individual, but in particular persons through various dispensations. In 1930 the Ruling Family was definitely not assimilated to the idea that self-determination was a right of the people. This was true also of members of the royal household, and of other shaikhs and their households. The tribal remnants in Bahrain had deep loyalties to traditional relationships. They accepted as a principle the right of the Ruling Family to make any and all decisions affecting the lives of their subjects, and were prepared if necessary to fight to the end in support of the Ruler's supreme authority. There were also considerable numbers of persons at the town-fringe and village level who, without the positive loyalties of the tribal groups, passively accepted their condition of social and political servitude as in the natural order of things, and if the idea of self-determination had been put up to them would have rejected it as a change from the security of the known to the insecurity of the unknown.

Even within the small mobilized segment of the population in 1930, there was little evidence of any concern for the right of self-determination so long as business went on as usual. Commercial practices were in tune with the times, and merchants were not interested in social and political reforms. It was only later, as increased capabilities and opportunities required wider freedom of action and greater security of contract and possession, that Bahrain's businessmen became assimilated to the idea of self-determination in matters of law and commercial practice.

So our brief preview of Bahrain society just before the awakening period of the early 1930's shows that although the concept of self-determination as a right existed within the framework of traditional institutions, there was not yet sufficient mobilization for social action to allow this idea to become an issue around which any massive reorganization could take place. The communication system was not yet capable of transmitting this kind of message on the necessary scale.

Our next step is to look again at the groups described, in 1940 and again in 1950, to see what significant changes took place during these two decades. The events of the 1930's can be recapitulated briefly. Belgrave introduced schools, administrative and public health reforms, roads, and other public services. The oil company provided employment, caused migrations of workers and their families, stimulated trade and other local economic activities, and introduced social and technological innovations of many kinds. Increased literacy, radios, and cinema houses provided new channels for communication both within the community and with the world outside, and new ideas flowed through these channels.

The most conspicuous result of these events was the rapid mobilization that took place. The newly mobilized group consisted mainly of merchants, oil-company employees, workers in various new activities stimulated by economic growth, and students. The remaining unmobilized group consisted mainly of the fishermen, pearl divers, and town-fringe inhabitants or outlying villagers not employed in new activities. This unmobilized population, however, probably still accounted for something like three-quarters of the total.

Despite the conspicuous expansion of the mobilized group, there was little evidence by the end of the 1930 decade of any substantial change in the groups assimilated to the principle of self-determination. This was perhaps to have been expected. The relatively large changes that had come about, bringing opportunities for improved living and the promise of more to come, had their origin in outside sources and came like a boon. The people were aroused to achieve new goals that appeared within grasp, but the very abundance of new opportunities distracted their attention from any new ideas of political or social freedom. No doubt it was during this general period of rapid mobilization that the seeds of assimilation to self-determination were sown, but the harvest was to come later when the reasons for valuing it were more clear.

Between 1940 and 1950 the economic and psychological disorders of World War II affected Bahrain in the same way as they did other marginally involved areas. The oil company and the British tightened their disciplines, thereby increasing the general tension. Vastly stepped-up economic activities brought in "agitators" and "organizers" of various stripes— some no doubt with Communist motives or tendencies, but most with the announced intentions of uniting "labor" against "capital," or of freeing "slaves" from "imperialists." German and Italian propaganda found many listeners. "Youth Clubs" of doubtful purpose were created. Strikes were instituted. Subversive pamphlets and posters became common.

By 1950 important shifts in our key groups had taken place. The mobilized segment, which in 1940 took in only about one-fourth of the population, burgeoned during the ensuing decade. By 1950 scarcely a village remained in Bahrain where criteria equivalent to those suggested by Deutsch would not indicate substantial mobilization. There was hardly a family that did not have at least one member employed by the oil company, the government, or some private firm serving these two major activities. Nor a family without at least one child in school. Every village had several radios, and propaganda programs went on twenty-four hours a day for those who wished to listen. Coffee shops buzzed with gossip and rumor about world as well as local events.

In short, by 1950 nearly the entire population of Bahrain had become mobilized.

But as we look at this shift we see that not all those who became mobilized also became assimilated to the nationalist movement; that is, not all embraced the right of self-determination as a principle. Nevertheless, assimilation to self-determination made substantial gains during the 1940's. Indeed, one of the most striking changes during this decade was the emergence of this assimilated group.

To prove that this change took place, we must look for indications that increasing numbers of persons began to find themselves in situations which either permitted or required that they choose for themselves between alternative courses of action as a means toward some goal. But the right to make such a choice must be qualified by the requirement that it also be enjoyed by others—that is, it is a social, not merely an individual right. Further, we must look for the exercise of this right in new, nontraditional situations as they come about in a changing society. Such evidence would support the conclusion that the right itself exists as a principle in the minds of the people and that men began to think for themselves in the growing belief that it is possible to modify their fate through the exercise of their own wills, rather than invariably to submit to patterns fixed by tradition or by other persons.

We see such evidence first in the new games the people of Bahrain began to play. The Arab people, generally speaking, are not traditionally a game-playing people. In traditional surroundings their leisure is spent typically in rest or conversation. But in Bahrain from the mid-1930's on, new games appeared in which both young and old took part either as participants or as spectators—games such as soccer, cricket, other field sports, and boat-racing, which entailed individual decision as well as adherence to rules and the decisions of others. These games began to fill more and more leisure time.

Teams and sports clubs were formed, each with its own rights and rules.

The right to travel took on meaning as methods of travel became available—the right to change one's surroundings, to widen one's world, to seek new sources of employment, to escape parochial restraints. The bus and the bicycle opened new doors through which one could pass if he chose. Their acceptance by the society connoted a right to their use.

Increasing literacy—noticed if not yet enjoyed by the masses—led to the expectation that books and newspapers would be read, and legitimized the right to read them. Listening to radio broadcasts and attending cinema shows also emerged as rights.

Many new opportunities for employment, opened by both the oil company and by government undertakings, implicitly legitimized individual decisions to depart from old ways and embrace new ones. Many of the new ways required individual decisions but placed limitations upon their kind and extent in order that a larger interest be served. A whole new set of rights and obligations became available to those who chose to embrace them. Thus the creation by the oil company of an Employees' Relations Department led to a new sense of rights of employees. New labor organizations—taxi drivers, oil workers—fostered similar rights with rules and regulations to safeguard them.

Clearly the people of Bahrain were opening their minds to new concepts of rights—but many of these new concepts did not necessarily have political significance. They were new social rights, the rights of an individual within the framework of a changing society.

But other new rights became evident which did have political significance. Among the people who had benefited from ten or fifteen years of change within the country, the realization grew that they now had something to protect, not only their present achievements but also their expectations for the future. There was a clear need for new institutions and for changes in the old ones. Popular criticism grew— criticisms of the Ruling Family for the special privileges it claimed; of the courts for discrimination and corruption; of the government for not pressing ahead faster with reforms and new services; and of the British for their alleged part in supporting outworn institutions and retarding progress.

Other significant evidence is seen in the sweeping restructuring of the Arab world that began with the close of the war in the middle 1940's. The restructuring was marked by the Arab-Israeli conflict, a succession of popular rebellions and government coups, the withdrawal of the British as the paramount power in several key Arab areas, American entrance as a political and strategic power of the first order, and a hard-pressed renewal of the movement toward Arab unity fostered mainly by Nasser. These events, though mainly external to Bahrain, had a deep effect there, particularly in the segment of the population that had become mobilized—sensitive to what went on around it. Out of this came many new ideas, regionwide but with repercussions in Bahrain. Arab nationalism, always present in a diffused form, was intensified by the conflict with Israel, and the Bahrainis took sides with their fellow Arabs. State nationalisms were also intensified, and Bahrainis supported nationalist leaders of their choice in other Arab countries—not always the same ones, but always against foreign intrusions. New issues were arising in the Arab world, about which the Arabs themselves had to make up their minds. These issues concerned both the Arab world and the several Arab states that composed it. Bahrain was one of those states.

Although the massive mobilization of nearly the entire Bahrain population was crucial to the events that followed, it was not outwardly manifested by any conspicuous activities in the early fifties, nor did it appear to forewarn casual observers of the imminence of a violent outbreak. Mobilization lit the fuse of rebellion but did not produce the explosion. The bomb had not yet been attached.

Mobilization, as the term is defined here, is not a mere stimulation of a society to action of any kind. It is a consequence of interacting factors that affect variously the structure, institutions, and dynamics of a society in such a way as to condition it for response to new ideas. In a manner of speaking, mobilization connects up the elements of a society for mass response or mass action, but does not itself energize the society. Conversely, an emotional excitation produced by a popular leader, or the psychological reaction to inflammatory propaganda, does not in itself mobilize the group it affects. But if that group has been mobilized for social action, such a stimulus may be highly effective in bringing about either assimilation to, or differentiation from, the idea toward which that stimulus was directed.

This is precisely the situation we find in Bahrain in the early fifties. The population had become highly mobilized, and the group that was assimilated to the nationalist movement (as indicated by acceptance of the principle of self-determination) had grown steadily but probably still accounted for not more than one-fourth of the total population. This one-fourth, to be sure, included many active and influential members of the community, such persons being more likely than others to break with any traditions that encumber them. But breaks with tradition do not necessarily involve violence. Such persons are likely also to give thought to what has already been won, and not to invite conflict without purpose. Violent outbreaks are ordinarily started by those who have the most to gain, not those who have the most to lose.

If we assume that nearly all of Bahrain's total population, now mobilized for social action, faced the choice of either assimilating with the nationalist-minded group or remaining disassociated from it, it becomes important to discover what factors determined that choice. To remain unassimilated to the right of self-determination might mean to remain without interest in that right or it might mean assimilation to an opposing idea. Within Bahrain the only organized opposition to popular self-determination was represented by the Ruling Family and its supporters—and toward 1950 some of its younger members seemed only half-hearted in their opposition. Even as late as the early fifties it might have been possible for the Ruling Family to win the adherence of the mobilized but "uncommitted" population to some acceptably modified traditional pattern of subservience to the will of the Ruler. But the measures actually taken by the Ruler, at least initially, had a contrary effect.

At this point we must reintroduce an element that had appeared in Bahrain's society during the decade of the forties, when mobilization made its great advance. These were the "agitators" and "organizers" of various stripes who undertook to stir the population or particular groups to action toward certain ends. The inherent right of the individual or of social groups to self-determination, subject to the provision that its exercise shall not infringe upon the similar rights of others, is not likely to have strong appeal as a political principle to an illiterate, impoverished, and traditionally subjugated population. But a popular leader who can point to specific and familiar instances of foreign domination, or of discrimination, oppression, or corruption on the part of the government administration, and exhort his listeners in the public mosque or coffee house to unite behind him to compel reforms, can stimulate large numbers to action under his leadership. If he guided them toward an organized group that was already assimilated to the doctrine of self-determination, these mobilized followers would assimilate to that group, or at least this is when their choice would have to be made.

In Bahrain during the early fifties one popular Arab leader emerged from the ranks of the people to stand out over the other agitators. He was Abdurahman Al Bekhir, who was born in the neighboring Shaikhdom of Qatar, became a Bahraini by adoption, and in the official opinion was a renegade from both, won over by Communist seduction.

Al Bekhir, held in detestation by the Ruling Family and in stern disapproval by British officials, addressed himself to the task of arousing the Bahrain population to rebel against their oppressions. He did not advocate violence; on the contrary, events showed him determined to avoid violence except as a last resort, and capable of controlling his followers except in a few instances of mob clashes with the police. But he did advocate exercising the united strength of the population as a threatening pressure upon the government to institute reforms of a kind that had the widespread support of the people. His actual demands upon the government, taken at their face value, were moderate, and in the privately expressed opinion of many responsible members of the community, the reforms he sought were long overdue. But his formidable organization of subleaders and committees plainly constituted an overt threat to the established authority of the Ruler, who flatly refused to treat with him or with the popular delegation through which the demands for reform were presented.

The first demands were for reform of the courts, including the replacement of certain magistrates who were members of the Arab elite but notably incompetent and corrupt by the Arabs' own standards. Popular representation was demanded at the legislative level through an elected council. Public participation in the administration of education and public-health affairs was also demanded. Failure to meet these demands, it was threatened, would bring on a general strike.

The Ruler refused to consider even a compromise settlement, on the joint grounds that progress toward the indicated goals was continuously being made and that no responsible Ruler could be expected to act under threats or in the face of insubordination. His continued refusal did in fact bring on a general strike in December 1954. It was skillfully planned and executed without public disorder and completely paralyzed the economy for one week, whereupon negotiations were again attempted by Al Bekhir and his committees, without result.

It is not necessary to detail the growing strife during the years 1954–1957, the increasing outbreaks of violence and the general rise of bitterness not always tempered with reason on either side. What concerns us is the fact that, partly under Al Bekhir's popular leadership but partly also because of support from the progressive business segment of the community, a widespread feeling developed that Bahrain should be for the Bahrainis—not for either a privileged elite or any foreign interests that looked upon it as a strategic or commercial outpost. Here, in short, we have the assimilation of a very large part of the total population—substantially all of it mobilized by now—to the doctrine of self-determination in both internal and external affairs.

We cannot carry this analysis beyond 1957, for clashes of increasing severity culminated in the arrival of British troops in November of that year and the suppression of rebellious activities. But enough has been said to show that the groups defined here were identifiable in Bahrain throughout the period of about twenty-five years just examined, and that the progressive redistribution of the total population among these groups was consistently related to the growth of nationalism during that period. To verify the assumption that this relationship is a causal one, that is, that nationalism is a *result* of mobilization, we must find that increasing mobilization precedes a rise in nationalism, rather than following or merely accompanying it. If we find also that there is no rise in nationalism when mobilization has not taken place, even though other factors usually associated with nationalism are present, the verification becomes stronger. In Bahrain we do find that mobilization rose to a peak considerably in advance of a rise in nationalism. We find also that in the earlier part of the period examined, that is, before mobilization had affected more than small numbers, the efforts of popular leaders to arouse the people and unite them in any concerted movement had only a transient effect with no indication that the concept of nationalism had been implanted. Instead, such efforts resulted only in limited and apparently aimless strikes and inconsequential clashes among factions.

The criticism might be made that the chain of events we have just traced in Bahrain could be explained equally plausibly as a case of a rebel leader inciting a mob to a series of fanatical acts, finally requiring only a stern exercise of discipline to restore the even course of law and order. That such emotional excitation did take place frequently in Bahrain cannot be questioned, nor that it was effective in producing certain events. It was due both to local leaders and to propaganda from Egypt, Iraq, and elsewhere. But the cumulative change that took place in the Bahrain society in the twenty-five years, say, from 1930 to 1955, was not reversible by any specific exercise of authority—even by British troops. It was a product of expanding social communications that progressively mobilized a population for *social*—not merely individual or traditional action. In these circumstances a new idea, if it finds a response in the people, does not burn itself out where it falls. It has an effect on the society as a whole—an effect that may be expressed by acceptance, rejection, or division.

Since mobilization for social action is not reversible except through the slow decay of a society, to the extent that mobilization has occurred we can expect continuing mass social response to new ideas. In Bahrain we can trace this response in the growing demand by the Bahrainis for the right to live their own lives in their own fashion. Through this common aim they identified themselves more strongly than before as one people, with the right to determine for itself what that fashion of life would be.

One important question now calls for our consideration. Self-determination implies choice among various possible fashions of life. But when a society begins to leave its traditional ways, and therefore when choice involves new ways that have no guiding associations with the past, *what determines choice?* This question confronts us whenever we try to understand some change that we see taking place within a society, or try to bring about some change.

The question is a broad one and involves many factors. What, for example, are the main factors that enter into a choice concerning how people will live when new ways are open to them—what they will eat, how they will dress, what work they will do and how they will do it, what old ways they will keep, what new ways they will seize, how they will behave toward one another? The choice which is relevant here is made by individual persons—even though affected by the society around them. These are factors that influence social change. Furthermore, what factors determine the restraints that are placed upon freedom of individual choice in order that self-determination may be equally available to all? That is, what is the source of authority, what determines its acceptability and how may it be transferred? What brings law and order into a society as it leaves its traditional ways? These factors can be said to concern political—as distinguished very roughly from social—change in a society as it emerges from a traditional past.

All of these factors must enter into a study of the changing Middle East. But to answer the question of what determines choice, we must examine first the motivations for both social and political change.

Chapter Six

Motivations for Social Change

"GROWTH IS the result of human effort. . . . Men are not likely to get more unless they try to get more." This observation by economist Arthur Lewis * might be challenged on the evidence of the vast oil wealth that has poured into Middle East countries and that seemed to provide a ready means of "getting more" without effort on the part of the people who received it. But such a challenge would be superficial. Lewis refers to economic growth within a society, and points to human effort as the mainspring of the growth process. His observation, taken in this sense, finds ample support in the Middle East. But it also gives us a starting point from which to examine motivation for social change.

In the earlier survey of the Middle East as a whole we saw evidence of change almost everywhere. In Bahrain we saw a society "mobilized" for change by expanding communications. The infusion of new ideas produced new desires and expectations and under their influence the society itself was

* Arthur Lewis, *The Theory of Economic Growth*. Homewood, Ill.: Richard D. Irwin, Inc., 1955. p. 23.

progressively restructured. But if men get more because they try to get more, we must look at the men themselves, for it is men—not societies—that want more. What more do men want? And what determines the effort they will make to get it?

My own observations have led to the conclusion that misunderstanding about what people want has been at the bottom of much of the difficulty in stimulating social change and growth in the Middle East. If we define social growth as a self-sustaining process through which desires stimulate effort and effort achieves satisfactions, what people want becomes a critical factor in determining the kind and rate of the growth that takes place.

Many Westerners and some Middle East leaders seem to believe that growth can be produced by providing "satisfactions" for which no desires exist. But this is true only to the extent that new desires are thus created. The salient fact is that effort is stimulated not by satisfactions but by desires.

We must now ask, *whose* desires are we talking about? Middle East leaders may want some things that are different from what their people want. Elite groups may have desires of their own. Some groups with modern ideas may want pretty much the same kinds of things that we do in the West. All these must be examined because they all influence growth. But what concerns us mainly here is what the underprivileged 75 to 90 percent of the population in most Middle East countries want as they leave their traditional ways and seek new goals. It is this aspect of the problem that is most obscure.

Much evidence supports the conclusion that the first things wanted by traditionally underprivileged people are not new things, but a sufficiency of familiar things. Quite generally, even the least privileged groups in an underdeveloped society have enjoyed—part of the time—an abundance of food, also freedom from disease, exposure, and other privations. Their first goals, as hopes are awakened, are most likely to be the same satisfactions more of the time, and then all the time. Also within underprivileged groups possessions are not evenly distributed; those with less want more of what they know others have and feel they lack.

This is not to say, of course, that they should not be induced to want new and different things—only that it *is* what they want that they will make an effort to get. Among the masses of the Middle East new wants typically follow upon each other in small steps, one leading to another. Let us look at some illustrations.

In 1947 I had occasion to travel over much of the back country of Turkey under the auspices of the Turkish government. On one excursion which took me into the northeast Anatolian region I schooled my interpreter to ask the same question in each of the twelve or fifteen relatively isolated villages that lay along our cross-country route. The question, put to the *khakodar* (head man), was: "What three things now lacking does your village want most?" The villages ranged from five to twenty or more families. In every village the men of the families engaged in a few minutes' clatter with the khakodar when the question was put. My interpreter took part to the extent of explaining that my purpose in asking the question was merely to find out for myself what the people regarded as most important for the good of the village. The answer in each case was given by the khakodar, without evidence of any dispute after he had spoken. In the first few villages I urged the interpreter to canvass the group for individual answers, but abandoned this after it became clear that none would be forthcoming. The interpreter explained that individual inquiries would be fruitless unless a far more intimate relationship were established than would be possible in a single visit.

In nearly all cases the first two choices were from the following groups: school-teachers, medical care, water for irrigation, and means of transportation. The third choice varied widely. The commonest were: a factory (as a source of employment for wages), tractors for agricultural use, cures for animal and plant diseases, and better houses. A few chose electricity.

If we take these answers at their face value, what desires or sense of need seem to lie back of them? A lack of irrigation water in a farming region characterized by periodic drought is explanation enough for a dependable water supply as a high-priority choice. But improved means of transportation in a practically roadless region which for many centuries got along with pack animals and bullock carts suggests that some change has taken place that gives transportation a new importance. This might be the discovery that a crop surplus over subsistence requirements could be moved to a cash market and that some desire could be satisfied if cash were available for exchange. High priority for the choice of medical care suggests a belief that modern techniques in that field are more efficacious than traditional remedies. The invariable first or second choice for school-teachers certainly indicates a new awareness of the importance of education and a desire that the oncoming generation fare better than the present one.

The answers were divided between those reflecting needs that were obvious, if familiar ways of life were to be improved—for example, medical care and water—and those reflecting concepts of new ways of life of which the people had become aware and to which they aspired. But none of them expressed directly what new way of life had become their goal; their expressed wants were for *means* toward goals which could only be inferred.

Another set of observations can be taken from the peasant uprising in Persian Azerbaijan in 1949. A succession of severe winters resulted in crop failures which left peasants not only without food to carry them through the winter of 1949–1950 but also without seed for planting wheat. A wide variety of new expectations that had been aroused by Persia's Seven-Year Plan had not been realized, and hope had given way to despair. Without seed for planting, plowing seemed useless and oxen were killed for food. Entire villages—men, women, and children—took the road toward the capital, Tehran, on foot, in demonstration of their needs. The government took action through the Seven-Year Plan Organization after many thousands of peasants had reached the outskirts of Tehran, and succeeded in reversing the march—largely by providing soup kitchens along the route and then closing them progressively from south to north. But the government also opened a vast area in the Moghan Steppe bordering the Aras River, hitherto occupied only by grazing tribes, plowed it and planted it in wheat. Distressed peasant villages migrated en masse to the Moghan and there became more dependent than ever on one another and upon the government. Without any of the familiar surroundings to which they were traditionally accustomed, including even the self-interested paternalism of their former landlords, they looked to the government for nearly everything—plowing by tractor, mechanical seeding and harvesting, water supply, and many new social services unknown to them before. The goal of better living came to the peasants almost without effort on their part.

My own observations did not extend beyond the first three years of this program, but during that time there was no evidence that this new and widely different life was looked upon as anything but a manifestation of fate, not associated in any way with the people's own capability for achievement. In their new circumstances the peasants seemed to be completely content. More than a decade has now passed and the Moghan development has been considerably extended under government direction. Here would be an opportunity to ob-

serve whether and how desire grows for what has been received in advance of a desire for it—the case of men getting
more without wanting more. Do desires that lag behind their
"satisfactions" still have the power to stimulate growth? Or
when desires have caught up with what has already been
provided, do they tend to fade and arrest growth at that level?

The two cases just sketched involve factors that influence
what groups of people want. But we can come closer to the
factors that determine what men want and the effort they will
make to get it through observations of individual men. We
can look at the case of Abdullah bin Mohammed in Bahrain,
for example. Abdullah had been trained for several years in
the storage battery shop of the oil company. He became dis-
satisfied with his wages, which no longer sufficed to meet the
growing desires of his family for the new consumer items that
were continually appearing in the market. The Company
proposed that he go into business for himself, opening a
battery-charging shop in Manama with equipment that the
Company would provide on easy terms. The number of automobiles in the local community was growing rapidly, and
the man decided to take this opportunity to increase his purchasing power. His new shop was immediately profitable and
additional goals were brought within reach. But the story
does not end here.

At that time distilled water for the batteries had to be
brought from the oil refinery, thirteen miles away, and so
brackish water from a nearby well began to be substituted—
and even a nearer supply from the sea was used unless Abdullah kept close watch on his helpers. Promises for early delivery
to his customers were kept by forcing the charging process at
rates that buckled the lead grids. Old electrolyte was reused
to save the cost of new. Customers fell away. I was among them,
for I found that I had to buy a complete set of new batteries
each year to keep our own island services operating. Competi-

tors moved in and Abdullah's business dropped to almost nothing. He asked the Company to take him back in his old job. But the shop foreman reminded him that, according to a familiar American advertising slogan—dubiously attributed to an Arab source—"the priceless ingredient of every product is the honor and integrity of its maker," and advised Abdullah to lay in a stock of this ingredient. I can report that he did change his ways, and that a few years later he turned a flourishing business over to his son and retired. Moreover, he had a shining electric refrigerator in each room of his simple *barasti,* well stocked with Pepsi-Cola for his grandchildren. This seemed to satisfy his highest material desires.

What is significant in these cases is not merely that men developed new desires—for better food, clothing, housing and various gadgets—that required cash from wages or profits as means to satisfy them; evidence of such growing desires is abundant, even though, as in the case of Abdullah the batteryman, there are limits to what men want enough to try to get it. Far more significant is the evidence that with new desires new values were put on the faithful performance of contract, fair dealings with employees and customers, new skills, and broader knowledge. These things became means through which the desires could be achieved. New values must have been put on them, because a price—in terms of effort and of giving up old values—had to be paid for them.

We can say that the value placed upon a given thing is what determines the desirability of that thing. The relation of one value to another determines what men want and will try to get. But it does not necessarily follow that each individual determines entirely for himself the value that is attached to a given thing. If this were so, to say that value determines desire would be mere tautology. Values are determined largely—perhaps even mainly—by something outside the individual himself. To discover what that "something" is, is an important part of determining motivation for change.

My own observations have suggested that substantial segments of the Middle East population place widely differing values upon identical things; and also that those values may be widely different from corresponding values prevailing in the West. This diversity makes it more difficult to understand Middle East value systems, but also makes it more important that they be understood. With insight into these values we can better understand how they influence behavior, and how in some cases behavior can be changed by changing the values which influence it.

My own way of identifying values as determinants of behavior—a completely empirical way—has been to observe differences in behavior of individuals or groups in comparable circumstances, and after making such allowances as I could for other influences, to attribute remaining differences to differing values. Thus, when I have seen a man from a respected family and of generally high repute deliberately conspire with others of his type to divert public funds into his own pocket, and when I note that this is done without visible shame or guilt on his part, and without loss of prestige among others who know about it, I conclude that the value placed by him and his kind upon what *we* call "honesty" or "civic responsibility" is not the same as ours. My conclusion is based not only on the conduct itself but also on the social sanctions that exist or do not exist in relation to it.

In somewhat the same way I have observed a propensity among most Middle East societies, but particularly among the Arabs, for people to say what they think their listeners would like to hear, regardless of what they know to be the literal fact. This has led me to the judgment that, in general, they place a lower value upon literal truth than is common in the West. We do not commonly abandon fact for fantasy— or at least we do not condone it in others—unless there is a clear reason for deception, as in our advertising, for example, where a higher value is placed on profit than on truth. The Arabs, too, may place a higher value upon something else than they do upon the literal truth. But that "something" appears to be different in their case than in ours.

I was once very anxious to talk with Shaikh Yousuf, a well-known Arab dignitary, and made repeated visits to the community where he lived to see him, only to find that he was away. On one such visit an intimate Arab friend said to me, "Shaikh Yousuf is not at home but he will be here on the fifth day from now." On the fifth day I returned. No Shaikh Yousuf. From various sources I learned that he had gone to India and had said that he would not be back for several months. I expressed my annoyance to my friend for misleading me, but I had not the heart to be annoyed at his guileless reply: "Yes, I knew that he had gone to India, but I knew how much you wished to see him—and now for five days you have been happy!"

Possibly the way a question is answered depends upon the relationship between the speakers—whether of the same religion or the same social class. Or perhaps it depends upon the content of the question and the right of the questioner to expect a truthful answer. I have had it explained to me that both Arabic and Persian are essentially languages of poetry and metaphor, and that one must look behind the words for the real message. Also it is said that repetition counts heavily in giving weight to truth—there are ninety-nine names for Allah, each one expressing a virtuous attribute. Once when our launch ran dry of fuel and left us drifting I chided our boatman for telling me before we started that he had filled the tank with petrol. He was aggrieved and answered, "But Sahib, I said it only once!" Clearly it was I who had let him down, by dropping the matter after only one answer.

Is the value placed upon literal truth simply an aspect of

the value on honesty and civic responsibility? It is difficult to answer this on observed evidence alone. My own experience leads me to believe that Westerners often stigmatize as "lies" what in the Middle East are only different ways of self-expression that are unfamiliar to us. To this extent, at least, the problem is one for the linguist rather than for the moralist.

Perhaps something about the value placed upon literal truth accounts in part for the general lack of interest throughout the Middle East in accurate statistics—and for the interest in inaccurate ones. I am almost sure that many of my friends in official positions in those countries have quite sincerely been more pleased with the figures they produced out of thin air for, say, cement production from state-owned factories, than they would have been with that actual production itself.

The very vagueness of these observations about values in the Middle East suggests the elusive nature of the concept of value itself—elusive at least, for the observer who seeks to capture it from empirical evidence alone. But from empirical evidence it would seem that values may be attached to *goals* that are sought as ends in themselves—health, leisure, prestige, security, gadgets of various kinds. Also that values may be attached to *means* through which such goals can be attained—effort, skills, shrewdness, supernatural forces, tools, and ways of doing things generally. There seems to be evidence also that values are attached to *attributes* such as qualities of character, charity, conformity, justice, and the like. But within the degree of refinement that is made possible by observation alone, attribute values can be classed as either *goal values* or *means values*.

I have already spoken of honesty. In Western societies generally, honesty, or integrity, is indoctrinated from early childhood as an objective attribute of character—a goal value.

This value as fixed by society rests upon a moral principle and is more or less absolute—not a matter of individual opinion. Individual conduct involving honesty is judged in relation to this standard; that is, we know when we are being dishonest. But in the Middle East it would seem that honesty as an objective attribute has been far more diversely valued than in the West. Traditionally, public officials have been most casual about what we would call honesty in their stewardship of public funds; so have merchants in their dealings with their clients. The intrinsic or goal value on honesty has been measured on a sliding scale. In recent years honesty has come to be regarded as a virtue in its own right, and lapses regarded as *dishonest* as they are generally in the West. The observer can note the change, but his observations do not tell him what brings it about.

When we turn from honesty as an objective virtue to honesty as a means of achieving a goal, we have other evidence to examine. We have seen that the means value on honesty can be raised merely by providing opportunities for goal achievement which, by the conditions imposed, make honesty a requirement. But in such cases is honesty valued as a means to a given end only in the same way that a wheelbarrow may be valued over a basket for carrying earth—but not, say, for carrying eggs? Or does a means value that proves its worth to the father become a goal value for the son?

Some persons appear to place a high value upon status as a goal. Such persons will make an effort to attain that status corresponding to the value in which it is held, and will sacrifice to this end what to them are lesser values. The status offered by social prestige has a high goal value in the Middle East. The Persian engineers who insisted upon making their relative positions in the Plan Organization conform with the standing of their families, rather than with their experience or their own opportunities for service or advancement, illustrate such a value. Another case is that of the Turkish foundry owner who wished to make only bronze propellers—"large ones, for large ships"—even though this spelled bankruptcy for his business. An output of railway brake-shoes and kitchenware, though profitable, was beneath the dignity of his family.

There is also much observable evidence that some persons place a high goal value upon being of *service* to the society of which they are a part, with no other visible reward than the approval of that society—or perhaps only the self-knowledge that a service has been performed. This motivating value is seen in the conduct of some reform-minded public officials, long-trained civil servants, teachers, philanthropists, doctors in rural areas, and in youth groups obsessed by socially oriented ideologies. The evidence seems to leave no other explanation for much of the conduct of such persons than that a high value is attached to serving others—friends, distressed classes, the nation.

One of the toughest problems facing medical doctors throughout the Middle East has long been the difficulty of creating a corps of competent women nurses. Women having the necessary educational qualifications usually belong to a highly status-minded class in the society. But the status of nursing is low. I have been assured by doctors of long experience that there is no shortage of young women who are not only qualified in every way for training as professional nurses, but who themselves place a high value on serving humanity. It is their families that object. Until the status of nursing at least approaches that in the West, Middle East doctors and hospitals must do the best they can with candidates drawn largely from the servant class.

The medical profession itself in the Middle East is not immune to the pressure of status. Like all other learned professions, it has high status value, and for this reason draws many to its ranks who do not place a corresponding value on service and achievement. Most professional men, including engineers, seem content to spend their lives in comfortable city quarters where status, rather than service or achievement, counts most.

There are many, however, who do place a high goal value upon achievement, even when visible rewards seem slight. The efforts made by some private businessmen, some public officials, doctors and teachers who choose to work in rural areas, and many people in racial or religious minority groups to whom high status is denied by social or legal discriminations, display conduct which is difficult to explain except on the assumption that achievement itself has high value. The obvious importance of such a motivational urge as a force in a developing society gives weight to two questions: what is the source of this value; and how can it be enhanced?

Recent work in psychology sheds some light on these questions. Professor David C. McClelland in a recent book * has reported results of clinical tests and field research which indicate that a particular and precisely defined psychological urge, which he calls *need for achievement,* exists in some individuals more than in others. He has also reached certain conclusions as to how this urge can be created or increased in people generally. Further, McClelland says that whatever the level of this urge to achieve in an individual or a society, it will not motivate persons to act unless an expectation has been aroused in them that some given course of action will satisfy this innate need for achievement. That is, although many other motivations can be induced by the hope of objective rewards—such as financial profit or social status—the urge to achieve for achievement's sake is aroused only by providing a goal against which achievement itself can be

---

* David C. McClelland, *The Achieving Society.* New York: D. Van Nostrand Co., 1961.

measured. This might be done, for example, by introducing the element of competition or of challenge, with some means of scoring success.

This raises a practical question. Among the various ways in which opportunities can be provided for men to get what they want—through aid programs or otherwise—which way most effectively arouses the urge to achieve? What are the conditions under which a goal value on achievement—at whatever level it exists—becomes an active motivational force? If, as the psychologists have said, this factor is crucial in stimulating effort, the practitioner—and particularly the policy-maker—should know the tests that aid programs should meet. The growth process depends largely upon effort.

Values based upon religious beliefs are especially perplexing to the observer. Quite generally among the Middle East peoples what is supernatural is valued more highly as a determinant in men's affairs than is the will of men themselves. But here we must distinguish between values that are based upon Islamic doctrine, and values based upon the folk religion, although the distinction may not always be clear.

Islamic doctrine fixes certain goal values as rewards in the next life for the trials suffered in this one. With these we are less concerned here. But Islamic doctrine also sets means values on ways that are to be followed here on earth. Doctrinally, these means values are objective and absolute—but, as explained in an earlier chapter, the means to which they apply are regarded as somewhat elastic. Values derived from the folk religion—the body of popular superstition concerning the supernatural—are another matter. They are not based upon doctrine, but upon cultural beliefs that in most cases long antedate Islam as a revealed religion. This distinction between doctrine and superstition, though obscure, is important, because folk religion crosses the borders of proclaimed faiths, particularly among the masses. Generally, among those of all faiths, the whims of *jinns* of many kinds matter more than the will of man.

However, the people themselves are beginning to distinguish the spiritual from the secular, and to revise their means values accordingly. Thus men learn that drought and loss of crops by disease or pest—once believed to be predestined (high value on doctrine) or the mischievous work of spirits (high value on superstition)—can be avoided by the use of irrigation and insecticides. Thus old means values on prayer, fetishes, and propitiations decline, and new means values are accepted. It may be that a somewhat similar change has taken place at a higher level of social organization, evidenced by the growing distinction between spiritual and secular sources of authority—for example in the separation of church and state which has taken place increasingly during the past generation in nearly all the Middle East countries.

Tradition is the most puzzling source of value that confronts the Middle East observer—the value on tradition itself, and tradition as a source of many other values. Tradition is an aspect of culture—the ways of life and the symbols which give meaning to life that are passed down from generation to generation within a society. That high value is given to tradition in a society which is only beginning to discover new ways of life follows from this definition. If values reflect a long-gone past that cannot be changed now, how can these values themselves be changed? Certainly not by changing the traditions that the values reflect, or by creating "new traditions." But, the practitioner asks, does the process of growth require that existing values be changed? Or only that *new* values— values upon innovations—be created that are more compelling in their effect than the old ones?

Innovation, as such, is not generally resisted by the Middle East peoples; on the whole it has high appeal. It is the *abandonment of tradition* that is resisted—the repudiation of a traditional value. If the policy-maker were more sure of this he could present innovation not as a repudiation of tradition, but as a new opportunity for choice. Old values need not be attacked. The positive approach is to demonstrate by whatever ways are feasible that the innovation has a higher value in whatever terms the people measure value.

From what has been said, it follows that goals are what people want and will make an effort to get. Goals are selected according to the values attached to them, and goal values generally are fixed by a people as an exercise of their right to say what those values are. Why certain goals are more highly valued than others is not always easy to know. Not even the people control this entirely for themselves. It is determined by what goes on around them, what is communicated to them from abroad, what has been transmitted to them from earlier generations, and the complex of personality factors that are attached to each individual as a human being.

But means values, in a real world, must be more rationally determined. Achievement of a given goal requires capability as well as effort, and capability is not determined—as effort is—by the desire of an individual.

The Middle East is rich in evidence that new goals are sought, and that the goal value on many of them is high. Most new goals, though not all, are innovations introduced by the West or modeled after Western patterns. As stated earlier, not all individuals or groups have the same goals, but most of the new goals that are highly valued in the Middle East are also highly valued in the West. But we are less concerned here with the values placed on goals than with the values placed on means—for although goal values may determine how much effort will be spent, means values determine *how* it will be spent. And effort without capability is likely to be both fruitless and frustrating.

Normally, capability of any kind does not develop far in advance of the use that is made of it or seen for it. In general, the greater the change represented by a new goal, the greater the number and diversity of the new capabilities that are necessary to achieve it. And unless a sufficiently high means value is placed upon the capabilities, they are not likely to be provided at all. Those who have never possessed such capabilities, or have never seen them demonstrated, are not likely to place a high enough value on them to choose them as the best ways to exercise effort. In such a case, inadequate means are quite likely to be chosen.

This is exactly what has taken place in many Middle East countries. Thus a goal of "industrialization" may be set and highly valued. But the change from a largely subsistence agricultural economy to one of high industrialization *requires* —for indisputable technical reasons—that many new capabilities be developed if industrialization is to be achieved and sustained. Some of the requisite capabilities can be provided from outside the society, for example through loans or technical aid. But there are other new capabilities which the society itself must provide through new institutions of many kinds, or which individual persons must possess. Except in a "police state," the people must first *want* to acquire these capabilities, for they are not come by without effort.

In the case of the peasant farmer whose highest priority goal is to produce enough food for his family even in years of drought or pest, a high means value on a pump or insecticides comes with his first knowledge of those means. But a high value on maintenance skill usually awaits a breakdown and the necessity of sending for a mechanic—and the difficulty in finding one. Abandoned machinery and shut-down factories all through the Middle East attest that the prevailing value upon skill in the operation and maintenance of modern equipment is low—not only at the peasant level but over the whole range of industrialization. Similarly, a high value on knowledge concerning the use of insecticides may have to await such an experience as that suffered by the silk producers in the Persian province of Mazanderan—where the DDT spray intended to kill flies and mosquitoes also killed the silkworms.

Even more difficult to establish are the values attached to less tangible capabilities, such as the administrative competence necessary to achieve increased national production. Prime Minister Menderes' early program of development in Turkey went well because almost every new capability that was provided helped to achieve some immediate goal independently of whatever else was done. During this period, say from 1946 to 1950, the economy was expanding as if into a vacuum. But a point was reached at which further achievements became interdependent—growth was no longer into a vacuum but into an existing economy of increasing complexity. New factories were dependent upon new power plants for their energy, new markets for their output, and new sources of trained personnel. Private undertakings were dependent in many ways upon what the government did or might do. Resources of many kinds required allocations based upon some consistent scale of priority. It was not a lack of anything upon which the Menderes regime itself placed a high value that made the program fail. It failed because the regime apparently placed no value at all—or only a low one —upon well-proved administrative means and methods without which similar projects would fail even in the West. Thus the regime simply did not want a coordinating staff that would have disclosed lacks and imbalances of many kinds before it was too late to correct them; and repeated offers from the West to help provide such a staff were rejected.

These are only a few examples of the way in which the values attached by the Middle East peoples to various goals and means affect their efforts toward modernization. Values may determine desires and desires may stimulate efforts—but are values the only motivations for the bewildering variety of behavior in the Middle East? Most observers long in the Middle East readily identify three types of behavior, usually, it is true, found in various combinations, but still recognizable as distinctive types. These can be referred to conveniently as *traditional, emotional,* and *reasoned.* This same typology has also been made by social scientists,* and this fact lends some weight to the observer's own distinctions.

The factor that is most significant to the policy-maker, however, is the susceptibility to change, by means available to him or to others, of these different types of behavior. Thus what he recognizes as traditional behavior, or a traditional aspect of behavior, which results from a deep-rooted urge to do as one's fathers have done, is little susceptible to change except over a long time and after considerable resistance. Emotional behavior results from psychological excitation of some kind—perhaps an inflammatory speech or radio broadcast. It is manifested by frenzied conduct, usually transient, and is little susceptible to change until its peak is past. Reasoned behavior results from a calculation of some kind which leads to a choice between alternative actions. It is susceptible to change by introducing some new factor into that choice.

Most of the actions that are based upon the values discussed previously have in them a strong element of reasoned behavior. This is because a person who consciously weighs one value against another—even a value based on tradition—and chooses between them, may be induced to make a different choice if a more desirable one is offered. The essence of

---

* Alexander Leighton, *Human Relations in a Changing World.* New York: Dutton & Co., 1949, p. 77. Also, S. F. Nadel, *Foundations of Social Anthropology.* London: Cohen and West, 1951, p. 30.

traditional behavior is conformity to a cultural pattern without recognition that choice outside that pattern is admissible. The important question is, of course, how can traditional behavior be converted to reasoned behavior, which is susceptible to controllable influences?

A question arises also in the case of emotional behavior, or the emotional aspect of an observed behavior. It may not always be feasible to wait until phrenetic conduct has subsided—a highly excited mob can work great damage in a short time. It may be possible to avert the dangerous peak of frenzy by timely moderation—but how?

Even reasoned behavior raises questions as to how it can be influenced. We must know what factors enter into the calculus of choice, and more or less how they are weighted, before we can decide what new factors can be introduced to change that choice. We have seen that in some cases we may be able to identify and appraise certain value factors as motivating or influencing behavior. But experience tells us that persons with different cultural backgrounds may have different systems of values; also that within a given culture, individuals differ in their responses to motivations of any kind; and that even a single individual will vary in his own response to a particular stimulus, depending upon what people surround him and his relationship to them.

Clearly, it is the relationships between these different types of behavior that is of paramount importance to the policymaker. But to understand fully these relationships would involve the terminology and principles used by social scientists in their analysis of behavioral problems, which may be unfamiliar to most policy-makers. No policy-maker concerned with problems of human behavior, however, can afford to overlook the work of the social scientists, and if the policymaker and the social scientist are to attack problems together, each must learn the other's language—at least up to a point.

This is not to say that a policy-maker need become a social scientist himself. But the nearer he can come to thinking about his particular problems in the terms that are used by social scientists in stating their general solutions, the more useful to him the work of social scientists is likely to be. Also, the more concepts he has concerning the behavior of people, the greater the possible range of his thinking about that behavior. The reason is clear. We think in concepts—the *meanings* attached to words. And for thinking about new things, new concepts are needed.

A perfect case in point is the difficulty in training supervisors everywhere in the Middle East. Supervisors of all kinds are needed at many levels of responsibility, but particularly at the lower levels where special technical knowledge is not a requirement—factory foremen, construction foremen, chief clerks, maintenance inspectors, and even "gang pushers" to supervise common labor. In the industrialized West—at least before automation—the foreman was the backbone of organization. He represented both management and labor, each to the other; interpreting orders from those above him, instructing those below him how to carry orders out, and seeing that the work got done. In typical American "personnel manuals" the qualities sought in a foreman are still indicated by such terms as leadership, reliability, fairness, resourcefulness, firmness, readiness to learn, enjoying the confidence and respect of his men, and so on. The qualifications of a general manager are described in very much the same terms. And pretty much the same qualities are found in both, because foremen become general managers. This is part of the reason why American industrial achievements have provided the pattern that is sought by most developing countries.

Typically, this "backbone" is missing in the Middle East; there is nothing between the head and the hands and feet. In any given undertaking the sheer necessity for supervisors

to guide untrained and mostly illiterate labor compels efforts
to produce them through foreman-training classes, on-the-job
training, and very often by mere trial and error. But the mag-
nitude of the need in an expanding economy requires that
the problem of producing foremen be examined more fully.
As an example, my own survey of Prime Minister Menderes'
program of development in Turkey in 1955 indicated that
even then there was dire need for something like ten times
as many competent foremen as existed in the country; and
new undertakings then projected would require as many
more. It was simply impossible to see where they would come
from through any efforts that were then being made to produce them. It is not only those who bear responsibility for the
execution of new works who are faced with this problem; a
large part of the educational systems in all the Middle East
countries is focused upon vocational needs, and foremanship
is a crucial need. Thus educators too are involved. How, then,
can supervisors be developed?

Surely Middle East values enter here as factors, some as
inducements to becoming foremen, some as obstacles in the
way. The value on status is an important factor. Most men
with education put a high value on status, but in their countries the status of the foreman is low—based upon the traditional image of a slave overseer. Class stratification puts a barrier between workers and those for whom they work—and
foremen are classed as workers. To tap the source of men best
qualified for foremen training thus requires that the status of
foremanship be raised. If men qualified for advancement to
higher posts could be induced to start as foremen, thus introducing vertical mobility into the organization from the
foreman level, the status of the job would tend to rise to the
level of the men who held it—as was said in connection with
nursing. But this merely restates the problem—how do we
get such men into the jobs?

Among Middle East workers themselves, status-seeking is not a compelling motivation. To them, status is fixed largely by tradition, particularly where authority is attached to status. Evidence described earlier suggests that at least among the Arabs of Bahrain and Saudi Arabia, men declined foremanship because according to their own sense of propriety no sufficient basis for the assertion of authority was provided by mere appointment to a foreman's job. In such a case, to further raise the status of foremen might only increase the reluctance to become foremen. Thus to draw men from the lower ranks for foreman training, the question is rather how to increase the value they place upon status, than how to raise the status of foremanship. Alternatively, values other than that on status might be exploited—a *means value* on foremanship because of higher wages, better quarters, less arduous work, and so on.

Practically speaking, the problem of developing foremen is one that involves individual men—not a society as a whole. Thus the question raised earlier—how can a value be changed?—now takes a different form: can a new value be impressed upon an individual independently of the prevailing value held by the society?

Because the problem of producing foremen is focused upon men as individuals, one great step forward would be made if attention could be concentrated upon the most promising individuals. In the West there are aptitude tests which vastly aid in the selection of candidates for training and promotion. For the Middle East generally no comparable tests have been developed. We need to know how to make such tests—but devising tests that disclose hidden traits and capabilities in individuals is beyond the normal capacity of the practitioner. If we could start with men who not only already value what is essential in good foremen, but who have mental and emotional qualities favorable for this type of work, the task of further training would become relatively simple.

But personality factors—whether values, personal traits, or aptitudes—are not the only ones involved in foremanship. A foreman is also a key member in a small social system within the larger surrounding one. The functional aspects of foremanship—interpretation and execution of orders, exercise of authority, instruction, mediation, and others—establish new relationships between the foreman and those around him. These new functional relationships may be quite different from the personal relationships with which both the foreman and those around him are familiar. It is an essential part of foreman training that these new relationships be explained—otherwise tensions and conflict are inevitable. But this understanding, in order to be taught to foremen, must first be understood by the teacher, and in the Middle East teachers capable of explaining such relationships are even more rare than good foremen.

Many years ago I had an opportunity to watch this social relationship factor operate in isolation from the Middle East environment. A Persian engineer came to the United States and after failing to find professional employment went to work as a laborer in an oil refinery where I too worked. For two years he urgently sought promotion through devices that he had learned at home, including gift-giving and attempts at bribery, until through sheer exasperation on the management's part he was promoted, on trial, to be foreman of his gang—a position he would have scorned in his own country but had learned to value in ours where its status was relatively high. The next day he showed up in his "store clothes" and exercised his new status by arrogantly shouting orders at his men, some of whom had college degrees and were working up from the bottom in the time-honored American way. The gang itself took care of his case, although until then he had been moderately popular. Before quitting-time he reported at the personnel office in a disheveled condition and indignantly resigned from the company. His own concept of foremanship, which implied *personal* superiority over others, was quite different from that of the Americans, who valued foremanship as a function. To them, the foreman acquired that value only by performing the function—not merely by occupying the post.

Thus the problem of developing an adequate supply of foremen in the Middle East countries involves more than the mere establishment of "foreman training" courses. We must know what constitutes "training" in theory as well as in practice. The situations that arise in a changing society can and must be studied in this way if they are to be resolved with any degree of success.

"The Middle East is the world's best testing ground for any and all theories relating to culture change over time," wrote W. D. Schorger, an American anthropologist.* "Culture change," as he uses the term, includes most of the changes that have taken place in the Middle East during the past quarter century. We reviewed some of them in the earlier chapters. But what are the theories to which he refers? And how are they to be tested?

In the paper from which this quotation was taken, Professor Schorger directs the attention of his social science colleagues to the importance of field studies along specific lines in the Middle East. "In actual practice," he says, "the conduct of anthropological research requires prolonged residence amongst the population whose culture is being studied. By the practice of techniques ranging from simple visual observation, through casual association, to the direct interro-

* W. D. Schorger, *A Frame of Reference for Anthropological Research on the Middle East.* Social Science Research Council, New York, 1957.

gation of informants, it is possible to accumulate data on the subject culture which can be crosschecked and which are also capable of verification by other and independent investigators."

This suggests that the practitioner who has prolonged residence and abundant opportunity for "simple visual observation" might play an important role as a collaborator with the anthropologist if only the communication between them were closer. Schorger's purpose in the paper is "to outline a general framework in which anthropological thinking and research on the area might be ordered." In his mind the real importance of such research is in the contribution it can make toward our understanding of what goes on around us. "In common with other sciences, and by which criterion it can be distinguished as a science, anthropological research is based on the premise that the behavior of natural phenomena is subject to regularities and follows patterns which, given precise enough conceptual and experimental instruments, can be isolated and defined. Once defined, these patterns of regularity can be utilized for the prediction of future behavior, whether it be in the realm of atomic fission or that of the response of Palestinian refugees to enforced indolence and poverty."

Schorger's observations concerning the need for research to discover "patterns of regularity" in Middle East behavior are broad enough to include not only research in the field of cultural systems, to which he refers specifically, but also in the fields of personality systems and social systems. The conventional designation of these three fields as those of anthropology, psychology, and sociology identifies these different approaches to behavioral theory—three areas of specialized study. But any given case of actual behavior involves all three of these systems simultaneously. Every person, that is, besides being an individual influenced by his own personality factors, is at the same time a member of some cultural system which has impressed its traditions upon him, and also of some social system which, through the interactions of individuals upon each other, likewise influences his behavior.

From the viewpoint of the practitioner faced with a perplexing situation, recognition of these three behavioral systems may help him identify the factors significant in that case. When he is faced with a traditional aspect of behavior, if he thinks of it in terms of the concepts which have already been linked together by the anthropological theory to which Schorger refers, he can view one part of the situation in those terms. He may not know what theories apply—but the anthropologist will, once he knows what the situation is. If the practitioner does no more than identify one part of his problem as involving cultural or traditional factors, this may be enough of a lead to get the help he needs—provided that the anthropologist himself has made the field studies that Schorger points out must be made.

Similarly, if the perplexity involves a difference in behavior among individuals even when the surrounding cultural and social conditions appear the same, what is significant is likely to be factors related to the personality system—many of which have already been reduced to orderly patterns by psychologists. To the extent that one part of the problem can be reduced to personality-system factors, at least a general solution may already have been found—but in any case we would know where to go for help.

Again, the common observation that a particular individual behaves in different ways depending upon what other persons surround him suggests that this aspect of his behavior involves social-system factors—the interaction between individuals. Sociologists have developed an extensive vocabulary of behavioral concepts, and the range of theory which relates them to one another is correspondingly wide. A single example, the *role theory*, will give some indication of how some general solutions to typical problems have already been found and are ready for application to particular cases—once the problem has been recognized and defined.

The role theory organizes one set of behavioral factors into a system within which sociologists generally agree that certain well-defined interactions take place. To state it simply, each actor—or member of a social system—sees himself in a certain *role* in respect to other actors, and is seen by them in a certain role in respect to themselves. Depending upon the role with which each actor identifies himself and others, certain expectations exist and influence behavior. That is, an actor's behavior will be influenced in part by what he believes is expected of him and in part by what he expects of others. This influence is modified in definite ways by other factors—for example whether or not a certain expectation is legitimate, or what sanctions might be imposed if an expectation is not met. This theory has been elaborated and extended to embrace a wide range of role systems corresponding to relationships that exist in actual societies.*

If the problems relating to motivation for social change in the Middle East are to be solved, they must first be defined in terms of the factors that are significant in each case. The solution is the discovery of the relationships that exist between those factors, so we know how a change in one will affect the others. At the least this will enable us to understand how changes take place, and in many cases it will enable us to produce a desired result by changing a controllable factor.

A practitioner or policy-maker confronted with the problem of change—whether to understand it or to produce it—must know what that problem is. He is not a social scientist,

---

* For a concise but illuminating discussion of theoretical background and an application of the role theory to an actual case, see *Explorations in Role Analysis* by Neal Gross *et al.* New York: John Wiley & Sons, 1958.

but if his work is with traditional societies he should at least possess what Edward A. Shils has said is the essence of sociology—an "imaginative feeling for the patterns of life and conduct of people whose ways are different from one's own." * If he has this, it is likely that he can identify the factors that are significant in a given case.

The social scientist cannot tell the practitioner which perplexing situations require analysis, though when he knows this he may help in identifying the significant factors. But he does have specialized techniques for investigating those factors and discovering their interrelations. In this sense he produces the general solutions which the practitioner applies to a particular case.

Although practitioners have need of more concepts to apply in the area of behavioral problems, and to enable them to communicate with social scientists concerning those problems, they should not be required to learn a different language for each social science. Social scientists can go much further than they have in the direction already laid out— by Talcott Parsons, Edward A. Shils, *et al.* for example †— in an effort to unify their terminology and integrate their theories. Practitioners would not be the only ones to benefit. In the physical sciences, for example, much of the advance that has been made has resulted from a unity of concepts which makes discoveries cumulative and enables hypotheses formulated in one field to be tested in another.

Most behavioral problems of importance to practitioners and policy-makers, moreover, can be discussed in plain English. True, basic concepts require words with precise meanings—but this does not necessitate a jargon intelligible only to high priests. Social scientists could perform a useful serv-

* Edward Shils, "On the Eve," *Twentieth Century.* Vol. 167, No. 999, May 1960, pp. 445–459.

† Talcott Parsons, Edward A. Shils, *et al. Toward a General Theory of Action.* Cambridge: Harvard University Press, 1951, p. 7.

ice by publishing more papers that are designed for policy-makers whose concern is with societies differing from our own. This would acquaint policy-makers with the concepts, principles, and techniques that are essential for sound analysis.

Also, if social scientists would give more thought to focusing their research on common sets of problems, where possible, instead of on separate and unrelated situations, their findings would have greater value. If research in their several fields were conducted in the same cultures, societies, or countries, many common factors could be canceled out, and significant relationships between different aspects of behavior would be disclosed. Obviously, this is not always practicable, but surely it is sometimes—far oftener than it is done. Even in the same field of specialized study, to work on unrelated projects seems to be the inexplainable rule rather than the explainable exception.

Further, if social scientists would make more effort from their side to learn what kinds of problems now face practitioners and policy-makers—granted that this is a mutual obligation—they could often serve their own aims by conducting their research in the context of those problems and at the same time put their knowledge to work.

And finally, social scientists, as teachers, could valuably devote part of their time to updating the present curricula in our schools, at all levels. The time to implant understanding of human behavior is certainly as early as that for studying salamanders and the Peloponnesian wars.

Chapter Seven

Motivations for Political Change

In the Middle East the political scene is the one most familiar to Westerners because of the headlines it has made. More importantly, it is the basis of law and order within a country, of allocations of national resources to various purposes, and of relations with the rest of the world. But the political structure of the Middle East has changed much over the last twenty-five or thirty years and is still changing. The "stop-camera" picture that the observer gets at a given instant is not the significant one, except as it shows a cross-section of history being made.

Changes in Middle East political systems confront the Westerner with many perplexing situations. For one thing, despite the antiquity of the region as a whole—that is, of its cultures—most of the present nations are new in the sense that their political systems are the product of sweeping new ideas of "modernization" which are transforming traditional societies wherever they exist. Most of these political changes are associated with the social change from traditional to non-traditional ways. But at this early level of national growth, what is the distinction between social and political change? Which one causes the other—or how are they related? In the West, political systems—like economic systems—have become highly institutionalized, and can perhaps be studied as independent systems of interacting political factors. But in the Middle East political behavior—at least in its early stages—is a particular manifestation of social behavior and can be subject to the same kind of analysis. What concerns us is how new political systems come into being in the first place, before elaboration and institutionalization have occurred.

If we say that the distinguishing characteristic of political behavior is the exercise of authority by some over others, just what are the factors that significantly influence the acceptability of that authority within a society as it moves from traditional to nontraditional ways? The search for these factors and their interrelations may prove endless, because neither social nor political evolution ever stops. But a good place to start is by briefly reviewing the Middle East political scene to provide a background for what can be observed directly.

In Turkey in the middle thirties Ataturk was rebuilding his country. His rule, completely dictatorial, was accepted by the Turks with loyalty and devotion as what they needed and wanted. Upon his death in 1938 he was succeeded by Inonu, who remained president for twelve years, until 1950. During this period the government continued to be completely authoritarian, but the real source of power shifted from Inonu as dictator to an oligarchy of traditionally elite families. This entrenched group used its all but complete control over economic resources, public communications, and police and military power very largely in its own political and economic interests. The constitutional policy of *étatisme,* or state control over economic resources and means of production, was continued, but the social aims that had given purpose to this policy under Ataturk were forgotten. Instead, exploitation of the national economy became, in effect, a highly organized private enterprise, restricted mainly to those with political influence, or parceled out as patronage for their support. Ataturk's foreign-built industrialization system, bereft of its foreign technicians since the outbreak of war, dropped to low gear and became little more than a payroll for political ends. His *halkevi* institution ("people's houses"), which reached into every village, changed from its original purpose as an instrument of cultural advancement to become part of the political machine. Private capital, always sensitive to political risk, was withdrawn from productive use, and was hoarded or exported for safety.

In these circumstances it was not surprising that the newly formed Democrat Party met resounding defeat in the 1946 elections. A bi-party political system does not work unless the votes cast for the opposition are counted, and the government displayed no intention that this would be done. As a result, substantial blocs of potential voters abstained from casting their ballots, remonstrating against the government for not permitting opposition representatives to participate in supervising the election.

An observer in Turkey during this period could have watched an early symptom of the revolutionary process which Crane Brinton has called "the desertion of the intellectuals." * It is worth pointing to here because it will be seen again—and not only in Turkey. During the late 1940's the writers, editors, teachers, and leaders generally of the educated segment of the society withdrew their support of the entrenched political group, and began to lay a foundation of

---

* Crane Brinton, *The Anatomy of Revolution*, revised edition. New York: Prentice-Hall, 1952, p. 45.

principles for social and political reforms. These principles had an even deeper foundation in the earlier Young Turk movement that had launched the Ataturk revolution but had almost been forgotten in the chaos of three wars and the bustle of national reconstruction. That movement was revived in the middle 1940's as a moral repudiation of the government policies that seemed to be carrying the New Turkey backward toward a class-ridden society of peasants and privileged elites. The Inonu government answered this intellectual revolt with stern measures. A clamp was put on the press, and crusading editors were jailed. Teachers who criticized the government were removed. Unfavorable books were banned.

Actions that closed channels of popular expression only hastened the opening of minds, particularly among the younger generation. The Democrat Party, under the vigorous leadership of its four founders,* provided a vehicle for giving this intellectual revolt political expression. It was supported by the business community for economic reasons, and by the peasantry as a hoped-for return to Ataturk's promised reforms. In 1950, Inonu, reading the signs rightly this time, allowed a free election to take place, and the Democrat Party went in on a landslide of popular votes. Adnan Menderes headed the government as Prime Minister.

This government was democratic in both name and nature. Its achievements during the first half of its decade in power were praiseworthy from all points of view. It was returned to power in 1954 with even a greater majority than before, and again in 1957—by dubious electoral manipulations. But its zeal finally exceeded its administrative capacity, and by the late fifties its excesses and failures in the eco-

---

* Celal Bayar, Adnan Menderes, Fuat Koprulu, and Refik Koraltan, who after the 1950 elections became respectively President of the Republic, Prime Minister, Foreign Minister, and President of the Grand National Assembly.

nomic sphere had brought the country to the very edge of collapse. Rising criticism was answered by suppression even more ruthless than that of the former regime, and again the intellectuals revolted, and suffered the same penalties as before—but they also opened minds, as before.

The climax came in 1959, when, with all other channels for popular expression closed by decree, the military moved in to rescue Turkey from the small handful of politicians who seemingly had lost their own way. Parliament was suspended, and the Army, under General Gursal, assumed authoritarian power pending new elections and restoration of parliamentary rule. New elections were held in October, 1961. General Gursal was made President. Inonu became Prime Minister.

It is not relevant here to pass a judgment on this method of solving a political problem. But the attitudes the Western observer meets in his talks with representative Turks are quite clear. Most intellectual and economic leaders among the people would have been glad to exchange the ostentatious shows of modernization that flourished under the Democrat regime for more enduring foundations for growth—individual freedom, preservation of the two-party political system, and confidence in economic policy. The popular masses are less articulate, but the goals they appear to seek—health, schools, rising opportunities, and freedom to make the most of these—are all compatible with the more sophisticated goals first named. The Turks are a tough-minded people, and their determination to move forward has become irreversible. One impression is inescapable: the goals toward which they are moving are regarded as inherent rights, not privileges to be bestowed or withheld by decree.

In Persia a review of recent political history would show a somewhat similar beginning, with Reza Shah as the Liberator, until his abdication with the outbreak of World War II. The country was then occupied by the Allies, and such national government as remained passed into the hands of a self-serving oligarchy of landed elite. Beginning in 1946, the young Shah Mohammed Reza Pahlavi made a start toward reforms. His Seven-Year Plan was interrupted by the suspension of oil revenues in 1951 after Mossadegh's rise to power. They were resumed three years later after Mossadegh had been displaced and new revenues had been established. But Reza Shah had lacked Ataturk's genius for creating viable institutions, political, social, and economic, and what little he left did not survive the Allied occupation as a foundation upon which the young Shah could build. Good intentions did not prove to be a substitute for a soundly conceived political system, and although the Constitution of 1906 remained nominally in force and parliamentary ceremonies were observed, by 1961 the Shah's frustrations seemed to have disillusioned him concerning his earlier concepts of democracy, of which little but the trappings remained.

Conspicuous in Persia today, as in Turkey on several critical occasions, is the desertion of the intellectuals, coupled with social and economic discontent. The intellectual has always held a high place in popular Persian esteem—in older times the poet and the scholar, now the teacher and the writer. Teachers and writers are multiplying, and many of them express concern over the lack of morality and national purpose in Persia's government today. Political nationalism has never been a Persian characteristic. Such unity as has bound Persia's diverse social elements together for twenty-five hundred years has been cultural rather than political. But political consciousness is growing as expanding communications break through geographic and social barriers, and when some catalyzing ideology takes hold, political nationalism may sweep Persia as it has other countries. There is little evidence that such a unifying ideology will crystallize out of the present political system. What strikes the Western observer as significant from the political point of view is the candor with which many Persians openly criticize the Shah and his favorites for their failure to carry out promised reforms, and for narrowing instead of broadening the group that benefits from national growth. The observer is struck also by the unconcealed popular view that American support of this narrowing group is mainly what keeps it in power. To foster these unfavorable opinions is the objective of Communist propaganda through continuous radio broadcasts, which, unhappily, are able to point to enough visible evidence to make even highly distorted interpretations seem plausible.

A visitor to Baghdad before the summer of 1958 would have found in Iraq such a government as his reading of most British and American newspapers had prepared him to find: constitutional, parliamentary, highly centralized, well-organized into departments staffed with capable British-trained civil servants, and seemingly so strongly entrenched as to defy both internal and external threats. Historically, it rested upon the Mandates following World War I. From these it had quickly developed into a parliamentary monarchy reigned over by a distinguished king from the Hashemite line (Protectors of the Holy Cities of Mecca and Medina), but ruled in fact by the British. Progressively over the years, although the influence of the British remained strong (as did their effective control over Iraq's oil and other resources), British political authority was relinquished to local hands. Nuri Pasha was perennial Prime Minister and, whether in or out of that office, was in effect the dictator of the country. Resentment against the British as imperialists, against the Hashemite Dynasty as intruders in eastern Arab affairs, and against Nuri Pasha as representing both, produced frequent popular rebel-

lions against the government. One of those rebellions, led by
Raschid Ali Al Gaillani in 1941, actually succeeded in taking
control of the government until put down by British troops.
But despite the seeming strength of Nuri Pasha's government,
an observant visitor in the early 1950's might have wondered,
as many did, whether anything but Nuri Pasha's strong control over the army maintained the government in power. It
could not have been popular support, for this did not exist,
nor was there any basis for popular support in social or economic reforms. But within the opposing political groups
leadership was divided—Nuri's deft hand showed here too—
and it remained for the younger army officers themselves,
under Colonel Kassem's leadership, to stage the bloody coup
of July, 1958. A visitor to Baghdad since that time, even the
most seasoned observer, might prudently withhold judgment
as to where the balance of internal political power does lie,
and in which direction it is likely to move. Several directions
are possible: toward or away from the Communist Bloc;
toward or away from the West; toward or away from other
Arab countries; or, if away from all the foregoing, toward an
independent "neutrality" or its own.

Among the other Arab countries, Egypt has the most clear-
cut political situation—a military dictatorship headed by
Nasser as an outgrowth of the 1952 rebellion against a corrupt and decadent monarchy. The constitution has been suspended (not for the first time) and only the shallowest pre-
tense is made of democratic political procedure. But frequent
government upsets notwithstanding, there is in the country
a long history of rule by law, established by generations of
British and French administration ever since Napoleon. With
this tradition, Nasser inherited a capable civil service, and
also an organized—if presently suppressed—political opposition. Nasser has survived politically by resorting to military

dictatorship, and his adroit use of foreign issues to keep his people united behind him. He has also assumed a leading role in the movement toward Arab unity. A step toward this was taken in the creation of the United Arab Republic by the union of Egypt and Syria in 1958, but was reversed by the Syrian revolt in 1961.

Social change since Nasser's rise to power—or since the days of the Pharaohs for that matter—has been little beyond what Nasser has done to redistribute the wealth of the country. Where this has been done, it has been by taking from the rich, both national and foreign, and giving to the poor. But most of it has gone to the poorest of all—the government itself, which even so has been saved from outright bankruptcy only by World Bank and American aid. Seizing factories and dividing land among peasants has not thus far increased the production of either. It is the distribution of production, not of unproductive capital, that satisfies consumers' wants. But since around 1958 Nasser has made fewer headlines and more reforms, and now that his government seems to have got what it wanted, the people's turn may come.

The Republic of Lebanon is governed by a revolving group of self-serving families, within which a precarious balance is maintained between the Moslem and Christian populations, which are about equal in numbers. Historically, Lebanon has been blessed with a population higher than Middle East average in industry and capability. Moreover, it is a compact country with natural advantages of many kinds. Class distinctions have been oppressive upon many, but even so the general standard of living has been relatively high for a Middle East country. The government, however, whether Ottoman, French, or Lebanese, has almost always been tolerated rather than supported by the people.

The other Arab countries can be dealt with more briefly. In Saudi Arabia King Saud maintains control with a combination of army power and tribal subsidies, while struggling with the problems of creating a departmentalized administration capable of taking the first steps toward economic and social modernization. In Jordan, King Husain faces similar problems, aggravated by angry Palestinian refugees, and also by an almost complete lack of resources, for which British and American support is an inadequate substitute. Yemen is still governed in its traditional way by its theocratic Imam; and the coastal Arab States (except Kuwait since 1961) are still subject to the protection and authority of the British, also to a variety of local stirrings toward rebellion and independence.

The analysis in Chapter 5 of the Bahrain rebellion as a "test tube" case indicated several significant factors which relate to both social and political change. One of these is social mobilization through effective means of communication, required for mass action within a society for either social or political purposes. Self-determination is another— the right of men to decide what they want; also assimilation to groups that want the same thing; and nationalism as a force uniting groups that want the same source of authority. Motivation, discussed in Chapter 6, also has relevance here— what stimulates men to act. To these factors we must add three new ones. The first is authority—a special manifestation of motivation through which the will of one man motivates another to act. And if we define government as the mechanism through which authority is exercised within a nation, we can identify from the historical evidence just reviewed two component mechanisms which must be included among our factors. These are survival mechanisms, which enable a government to retain authority in the face of aggression or revolt; and achievement mechanisms, which enable it to gain popular acceptability by giving the people what they want, or enabling them to get it. These factors, of course, are not the only ones that may have significance in any given situation. But those named—social mobilization, self-determination, assimilation, nationalism, motivation, authority, survival mechanisms, and achievement mechanisms—provide a basis for examining the connection between social change and political change. Each of them can be recognized not merely in books but in Middle Eastern events.

Widespread social mobilization was achieved in Turkey by Ataturk in the early 1930's and except for a few remote enclaves has remained complete since that time. In Persia, mobilization is high in or near the cities and towns, generally low in the rural districts, and scarcely evident in the tribal areas except in their fringes. In Iraq the same can be said, with the qualification that more of its people are concentrated around the few main centers; in the rural and tribal areas mobilization is low. This is generally true also for Syria and Jordan. Lebanon, except for a few fringe districts, is practically fully mobilized.

In all of these countries mobilization as it now exists took place chiefly in two periods, with variations in some cases. These were the periods immediately following the first and the second World Wars. The first period was marked by Ataturk, Reza Shah, and the Mandates; the second by widespread introduction of the radio, and a diversity of foreign activities in the Middle East, both commercial and military. The point of significance here is that the segments of the populations which were not mobilized during these two periods have changed little in this respect at other times—that is, relatively little has been done within those countries themselves to improve or increase the means which effect mobilization.

In the remaining countries mobilization has been more subject to local circumstances. In Egypt, despite the high concentration of its population along the Nile—always a great highway for social intercourse both within the society and with foreign countries—probably not more than half the population would have met the tests of mobilization until after the overthrow of the monarchy in 1952. Under British administration, high social mobilization was never an aim. It used to be said that a whisper in Khartoum could be heard in Port Said—and the "bazaar telegraph" throughout the Middle East does seem to be magic—but the kinds of messages that it can transmit are limited. Since Nasser's time the acoustics have been improved by modern means and it is probably true that a whisper anywhere in Egypt is heard in the central police office. It is also true that mobilization has become practically complete.

Saudi Arabia has become highly mobilized in its few main cities and in the oil region in the eastern province, since the oil operations became important and largely as a result of them. Kuwait and Bahrain also became mobilized rapidly after their oil activities got well under way—in Bahrain between 1940 and 1950, and in Kuwait somewhat later. In Yemen and the other coastal shaikhdoms mobilization is just beginning. In general it can be said that the various media through which ideas are communicated between and within societies have expanded so rapidly during the last few years that within another few years every part of the Middle East will have become mobilized for social action—for whatever influence this factor has upon both social and political change.

As for self-determination, what was said about its origins and its spread with increased mobilization in Bahrain applies generally to the other Middle East countries. Assimilation to new ideas—and to groups holding those ideas—has also operated regionwide in the same way that was described for

Bahrain, although the ideas have been more diverse and many kinds of new groups have been formed, each with its own leadership. Intellectual groups have assumed both social and political importance in Turkey, Persia, Syria, Lebanon, and Egypt; and somewhat less in Iraq. Entrepreneurial groups, both public and private, have grown rapidly—mainly in the countries just named—and provided a source of new efforts to increase production by new methods. Also in the broader picture, religious groups have greater importance than they were seen to have in Bahrain. In Turkey they were important enough to be eliminated by Ataturk early in his regime, and have been slow in returning. In Persia nearly the entire population is Shia Moslem. This avoids one source of internal tension which Iraq, divided between Sunni and Shia, or Lebanon, divided between Moslem and Christian, cannot escape. Other large groups have assimilated to new ideologies—Communism, democracy, neutrality; and still others to growing concepts of political parties. But the assimilation which has been most conspicuous in the last few decades throughout the Middle East is, as in the case of Bahrain, assimilation to the concept of nationalism.

By including *motivation* as a significant factor in relating social to political change, we are simply recognizing that what men want and the effort that they will make to get it—whether in the social or political field—depends upon a combination of cultural, personality, and social factors as discussed in the preceding chapter. What these separate factors are and how they are combined in any given situation depends upon what group of men we are looking at. In the present context the groups that concern us are those which have been united by agreement concerning a particular aspect of social or political change. Thus we can disregard a group that is united by racial affinity or a common religion, if the group affinity concerns neither social nor political change.

But if what unites the group is a desire to produce or resist such a change, we want to know the origin and intensity of the motivation so we can evaluate its influence.

Authority is evidenced in many ways. Here we need say only enough about it to enable its identification and evaluation in the actual situations that we shall look at to see how all these factors combine. But even for this we must expand somewhat the Bahrain explanation of the way in which the principle of self-determination operates to produce new groups through assimilation to that particular concept of a right.

Both in Bahrain and in the Middle East as a whole evidence shows that the principle of self-determination is a dual one. It combines two concepts—that of an individual right and that of a group right. That is, the exercise of the right by one person must not prevent its exercise by other members of the group. To safeguard the right for the group, therefore, sanctions must also be agreed upon by the group as a means of restraining transgressors—"those wise restraints that make freedom possible." Thus the principle of self-determination implicitly necessitates authority to exercise sanctions. But how is such a group formed? And what determines the nature and scope of the authority that exercises sanctions?

Here we can use the social scientists' concept of a social system, defined simply as a group of persons interacting in response to a common situation. There can be as many social systems as there are common situations to identify them. These groups may be overlapping. Thus a given individual may belong at the same time to a religious group including several races, a racial group including several religions, and a village or an occupational group including all of these. In each such case the group is likely to assert the group-right of self-determination in respect to the particular common attribute that identifies it as a group. To the extent that it does so, it becomes assimilated to the more embracing social system identified by a belief in that right. Thus a religious group may, by its own consensus, fix certain sanctions that impose restraints upon its members in respect to ritual observances, but at the same time accept sanctions fixed by consensus within the more embracing social system to prevent that religious group from imposing its own rituals upon nonmembers. In return, the religious group is protected by necessary sanctions against impositions by other groups.

We can trace the ascending system of authority through which sanctions are exercised throughout the entire social system that is identified by its common belief in the self-determination principle. We start with the individual—who for this purpose can be taken as a special case of a social "group," having the right of self-determination in matters that concern him alone. The sanctions which put a limit on his freedom in such matters may be only shame or guilt imposed by his own conscience.

Within groups of individuals, shame and guilt may again be among the sanctions available, but there are additional ones such as ostracism, expulsion, loss of possessions, and physical punishment. These are imposed—or at least legitimized —in each case by the consensus that affirms group rights. Thus the members of a family, severally, may have wide freedom in determining many aspects of their conduct, but the transgression by one member upon the rights of another is subject to the sanctions that, by consensus both within the family and among families, may be imposed by the head of that family. But to insure that those rights may be enjoyed within all families, all heads of families join in a consensus at the village or tribal level that their respective families will observe the rights of other families, and that sanctions to insure this may be imposed at the village or tribal level; and so with each successive widening of the social system.

The outermost boundary that could be drawn to include all the groups identified by a consensus as to their rights of self-determination would be a wide one, embracing a large part of the world's population. But what concerns us here is the outermost boundary that can be drawn to include those groups that have also joined a consensus as to what sanctions may be imposed upon them. This boundary is much more restricted.

For one thing, all the groups enclosed within the outermost boundary, whatever their affinitive attributes—that is, whether racial, linguistic, occupational, ideological, or other—accept the sanctions derived from consensus within that boundary. They do so to safeguard their own several rights against transgression, by jointly guaranteeing group-freedom for all. And since sanctions are legitimized by the same consensus that recognizes rights, it follows that no group within the boundary can accept authority that has its source outside the boundary. If it did so, the rights would become mere privileges to be granted or withheld by that external authority.

What has just been described must be regarded only as a model—a simplified representation of reality divested of all attributes and influences except those explicitly defined for it. But a model has its uses. This one represents the familiar concept of a sovereign nation—a collectivity of social systems with completely self-determined rights and sanction powers. The sanction powers representing authority comprise the national political system. The mechanisms through which authority is made effective represent government. And since both the rights and the sanction powers delimited by the defined boundary are determined by popular consensus, the nation thus created represents our concept of a social and political democracy.

What makes the model, as described, a democracy is the presumption that authority conferred by consensus can be rescinded by consensus. If, instead of this, authority should be seized and held by a group without regard for consensus, the political system would become authoritarian—or, if controlled by a single individual, a dictatorship. Or if authority were exercised by a foreign power the extended political system would represent our concept of imperialism. And if a prevailing consensus self-willed that the right of self-determination be subrogated to the state, that is, that only the state can legitimize rights and sanctions, the model would represent one aspect of the Communist doctrine—as asserted by Communist doctrinaires. These variant forms that the model might take are mentioned here only in passing, to show how various types of political systems are related to our model of a democracy.

To see how the factors just discussed have actually combined in reality, and with what consequences, we must turn from the model to the observed evidence. Surprisingly, perhaps, it is among the least advanced segments of Middle East society that political systems most closely approach the democracy represented by the theoretical model. This observation has frequently been made by observers of tribal societies, which have been described as more "democratic" than most Western societies. I have felt this many times myself. The first time was on an early visit to Riyadh, capital of Saudi Arabia. I sat by the King, Ibn Saud, in his *majlis* hall, with shaikhs and other dignitaries lining the walls in silent attendance. A *bedu* from the desert would stride through the door, unannounced, walk straight to the King, kiss his hand as a sign of fealty—then look him squarely in the eye and state his complaint, his request, or even his demand. Clearly, the King was *his* King—and directly accessible. But such democracies are also the lowest in an array based upon achieved social and economic advancement. Democracy, that is, does not necessarily produce social growth. Quite generally, in fact, when traditional motivations prevail in the society, the more the democracy the less the social change. People who do not want change are not likely to demand it of their government even though they have the power to do so. In most distinctly tribal societies, such as in the coastal Arab shaikhdoms, Yemen, the roving tribes of Iraq and Syria, and the Kurds, authority for the exercise of political—as distinguished from religious—authority within the tribe has not descended by inheritance. More often than not it has remained within the same family or group of families, but top authority is conferred traditionally by popular acclamation. Also traditionally, it can be rescinded legitimately by consensus, through whatever means are necessary—not excluding assassination. This is a robust form of democracy, but for those who want democracy for its own sake—here it is.

As soon as we turn toward countries that have made substantial changes in the direction of modernization, the political systems begin to show significant departures from the theoretical model, particularly as to the source of authority upon which sanction powers are based. Progressively, as mobilization proceeds and new ideas are spread, the source of authority as depicted by the model shifts away from the older group consensus toward a new consensus growing from new groups. The evidence on this point is inescapable, although its interpretation is not always simple. At whatever country we look, mobilization of any segment of the national population is followed by new desires, new efforts to satisfy them, new groups with common purposes, and new leadership with new authority over those groups.

We saw this in the Bahrain case. It has been going on in Saudi Arabia for more than a decade—with new leaders like the Crown Prince Faisal and Shaikh Abdullah Teriki drawing new group consensus toward them, even away from the King himself. It took place in Turkey during Ataturk's rise to power; and again during the 1940's as an entrepreneurial "middle class" grew and gave consensus support to Menderes and other leaders who—for a time—shared their aspirations for production through private enterprise. In Turkey also, new groups were formed during the same period within the rural population, with group aims for better living. They supported new leaders who shared in the new aims, and opposed the old leaders—even Inonu himself, although he was an almost legendary national hero. In Persia the spurt of mobilization after World War II, even though limited mainly to urbanized communities, was followed by the emergence of new groups formed around a diversity of new ideas and aims, each with its own leadership. Examples, identified here by conspicuous leaders, are: Ebtehaj for the Seven-Year Plan; Mossadegh for social and political reforms; Kashani for religious zealots; Makki for expulsion of foreigners; the Tudeh Party for Communism; and various intellectuals for freedom of thought and speech. Most of these group aims were independent of each other, but one thing was common among them: each asserted its right to determine and to strive for its own goals. Consensus on this point—dubious in the case of the Tudeh Party—led to a coalition of the groups with Mossadegh as the leader among leaders. The means first agreed upon as essential to all group aims was the overthrow of the old regime, whose authority no longer had consensus support. Overthrow achieved, the coalition fell apart—but this takes us beyond our present focus.

Here we may pause in our review of the evidence, and see what relationships seem to exist among the various factors under examination. Expanding channels of communication lead to mobilization and to social action in response to new desires. The values placed on goals and means determine, in part, motivation for action, which is also influenced by how the society is structured—the relationships among its members, and the fixed institutions that guide behavior. New ideas that are held in common bring about new groups. Self-determination, as one such idea, leads to the assimilation of all groups that accept this principle, and thus to an expanding acceptance of authority for the exercise of sanctions, and to nationalism. New authority tends to conflict with old, because the consensus upon which it rests is that of new groupings based on new ideas and goals.

This statement of relationships between these factors is a very general one indeed. But it does indicate what to look for in a given situation. In the Middle East there are many situations to which these generalizations can be applied. In different situations different factors have greater significance. One situation of importance is presented by the growth of nationalism and its influence in creating new nations or changing the boundaries of old ones. What are the factors, and their interactions, that determine the way nationalism works and how it affects political change?

It will be recalled that the theoretical model used earlier showed how proliferating groups that asserted group-rights led to an expanding system of sanctions to safeguard the rights of all. And also that a nation was defined as the largest collectivity of such groups that accepted sanctions based on common consensus but rejected sanctions based on authority external to that consensus. But it is unrealistic to suppose that this idealized situation exists in any real Middle East nation. That is, groups that accept sanction authority not arising from national consensus do exist in all Middle East countries. To the extent that this is so, their sovereignty is impaired. Conflicts are inevitable in such cases, between the different authorities, between one authority and the groups which look elsewhere for protective sanctions, and between groups which support different authorities. What form have such conflicts taken, and how have they been resolved?

In the Bahrain case sovereignty has never existed, because of the "paramount power" of the British. But in a closely parallel case, that of Kuwait, British authority has been formally withdrawn and—at least from that standpoint —Kuwait has attained sovereignty.

But there are many other kinds of cases to look at. In all the Middle East countries there are religious groups, such as the Sunni and Shia sects of the Moslems. The principle of self-determination is strongly supported by both. Each claims for itself and affirms for the other the distinctive rights of the sects, and both accept sanctions derived from and exercised by the political system of Islam which extends far beyond the boundary of the nation. Both groups, as Sunni and as Shia, or together as Moslem, must be excluded from the political system of the nation if its sovereignty is not to be impaired. This is true, at least, to the extent that Islam continues to exercise secular authority. Since the Caliphate was abolished in the early 1920's formal mechanisms of Islamic political authority have been largely extinguished, but many Islamic secular laws are still accepted widely by consensus.

In Turkey this requirement of sovereignty was met by a complete separation of church and state—in fact, by almost complete extinction of religion itself as a social institution within that country. In Saudi Arabia we see an opposite course: the state became theocratic, with Ibn Saud at the head of the only Islamic sect that mattered in political affairs. Even then sovereignty was less than complete, as witness the classic story of his difficulty in persuading the *ulema* to permit the installation of telephones in the country. The King resourcefully met the difficulty by demonstrating that the Koran could be read in at one end and come out undefiled at the other, thus proving that the telephone was not an instrument of *Shaitan* (the Devil).

Religious groups are not the only ones that may accept external authority for sanctions. Any group based upon a common situation which extends beyond national borders is in this class. Any racial, linguistic, occupational, or ideological enclave may be such a group, and to the extent that an external authority intrudes upon the national political system, sovereignty is impaired.

The argument is not made here that in no case *should* sovereignty be thus impaired. Sovereignty, too greatly fragmented, may not be viable in the real world. The point here is only that conflicts will develop if divergent consensuses exist as to what authority for sanctions is legitimate. Sociologists have said that, in general, a social system will tend to interact within itself in a way that will minimize internal stresses; this has been described also as a tendency to reduce group tension, or dissonance. The idealized model described earlier exhibited minimum internal stress—at least of political significance—because the social system (based upon rights) and the political system (based upon sanctions), having been created by the same consensus, were coextensive and completely congruent. But what we find in reality may be a single social system divided between two or more political systems, or several social systems with no common consensus as to sanctions existing under a single political system.

This gives us another way in which to define nationalism —that is, as the urge to make social system and political system coincident.

Ataturk first created a political system out of the resources available to him after World War I and the Greek war, and then proceeded to bring the Turkish social system into congruence with that political system by vigorous Procrustean methods that included exiling and annihilating Greeks, Jews, and Armenians. Continuing congruence was achieved by molding a new Turkish social consensus in keeping with political developments. The Turkish people have maintained stiff resistance to all subsequent intrusions of sanction power —whether by religion, ideologies, or renewed capitulations in any form. Turkish nationalism came at a high price, by Western standards of conduct, but it is the strongest observable force in Turkey.

The district of Alexandretta, peopled by Turks and formerly an Ottoman province, was placed by the Allies under the political system of the Syrian Mandate—a highly disparate combination of social and political systems. At the insistence of the people of Alexandretta their nationhood was restored by returning them to Turkey.

Another illustration of nationalism at work is seen in the separation of Lebanon and Syria after their liberation from French (Vichy) control during the Second World War. Under earlier Ottoman control they had long been regarded as separate *vilayets*. But under the Mandate, although they retained their own self-identification as separate social systems, the French political administration was in fact a single one. This led to high dissatisfaction among both Lebanese and Syrians, each accusing the other of self-serving use of authority. Neither was wholly right, since the French took advantage of them both impartially. As an intellectual influence the French left their mark on both societies, as they have on many others; but teaching shepherds to recite Molière and Racine instead of Firdowsi and Hafiz furnishes an insecure foundation upon which to build a new social-system consensus.

The Lebanese sought their own political system. The inhabitants of this coastal strip constituted a social-system enclave that had become differentiated from the Arab hinterland society as a result of ages of foreign trading and its long history as a battleground for Persians, Greeks, Arabs, Turks, and European Crusaders. The many centuries of intercourse with the outside world and of serving as a crossroads had created an unusual ethnic mixture; and this ethnic hetero-geneity, by differentiating the Lebanese from their Arab neighbors, had become more unifying than dividing. Lebanon had long been divided also on religious lines between two major social systems—Moslem and Christian—but a Leba-nese consensus had always recognized the rights of each "to live its own life in its own fashion," subject to the sanctions of whatever political system embraced both.

As opposed to this situation, the "Syria" created by the Mandate, not counting the part detached as Lebanon, was widely differentiated within itself. It contained the sophis-ticated merchant-city of Damascus, a segment of which had much in common with Lebanon and might even be regarded as belonging to the same social system, and also roving desert tribes and fiercely self-identified religious and racial minor-ities. Nevertheless, most of Syria's inhabitants regarded them-selves as "Arabs." During the period of the First World War and immediately after, much of the leadership in the Arab unification movement came from Syria. Although the desire for liberation from foreign political domination can be as-sumed to have been just as strong among the Syrians as among the Lebanese, there is reason to believe that Syrians might have accepted a broader Arab alliance instead of separate statehood if this choice had then been available to them. Arab nationalism, that is, approached and may even have exceeded Syrian nationalism as of that time.

In the actual event, the Lebanese people got their own political system when the Allies ousted the Vichy French in 1943. As for the composite "nation" contrived by the Allied Mandate as "Syria," it was left to find a compatible political system of its own—which at the time of this writing it is still seeking after nearly twenty years of trial and error. One experiment resulted in the union of Syria and Egypt in 1958 to form the United Arab Republic. To some Syrians this was an expression of Arab nationalism—Arabia irredenta, but to other Syrians it was a clear case of foreign domination by Egypt. It was terminated in 1961 by the action of a strongly Syrian nationalist group.

Nationalism is seen again in the assimilation of Arab Palestine to the political system of Transjordan to form the Kingdom of Jordan in 1948. Urbanized Palestinian Arabs in Jaffa and Haifa and the coastal strip between had more in common with the Lebanese than with the hinterland tribes, and if free to choose might have associated themselves with the Lebanese political system rather than that of Transjordan. But more generally the Palestine Arabs and the Transjordan Arabs were indistinguishable, and on the basis of many common aims and beliefs could be regarded as belonging to a single social system. To embrace the same political system, therefore, is precisely what was to be expected, once the exercise of sanctions in Palestine had been surrendered by the British.

Another instance of nationalism at work is seen in the creation of the Federated Arab States (Iraq and Jordan) closely following the formation of the United Arab Republic—but lasting only until the Kassem coup in Iraq. Still another is the progressive integration of the territorially undefined shaikhdoms of the Aden and Hadhramaut Protectorates, guided by the British but with what final results remains to be seen. Also worth noting are the various movements to form a "Greater Syria" by creating a single political system for the peoples of the "fertile crescent"—none of which movements succeeded, but all of which evidenced the urge of nationalism.

But not all clearly defined social systems, however strongly self-identified as autonomous nations by right, have yet been able to establish even group rights within an embracing political system, much less a national political system of their own. The Kurdish tribes comprise such a case. The Kurds have regarded themselves as a distinct social system for almost as far back as history goes, but their plea for a corresponding political system was rejected by the Allies at the close of World War I. Three and a half to five million of them— or perhaps even more, as variously estimated—are divided among five sovereign nations: Iraq, Syria, Turkey, Persia, and the Soviet Union. Traditional rights affirmed by their own consensus, as Kurds, include that of resolving internal conflicts by applying sanction authority in ways that are too hardy for Western tastes—raids, blood feuds, and the like—and this has given an impression abroad that the Kurds are not nation-minded.

But I can illustrate an aspect of Kurdish social-system consensus by a personal experience during a trip through their territory a few years ago. A local tribal chief who was our host for the night was explaining to my escort and interpreter how the Kurds felt about one another and the outside world. "We have an old saying among us," he told the interpreter, "that goes like this:

> I and my tribe against the world,
> I and my cousins against my tribe,
> I and my brothers against my cousins, and
> I against my brothers!"

As an expression of the right of self-determination in progressively more inclusive social systems, stated here in their diminishing order, this can hardly be improved upon. As for the Kurds' relations with the outside world, light was thrown on this in another way. In the course of the conversations that went on that evening I heard myself referred to at various times as the "rumi." The next day I asked my Kurdish escort what this meant. "A long time ago," he explained, with a smile, "the Romans, or rumi, invaded us from the West, and we have always used the same word for those who followed them!" This made it clear. They were Kurds. I was *rumi*.

These are illustrations of social systems seeking a change in the political system to which they are subject. But frequently nationalism is expressed by resisting such a change. Such resistance was present in Syria, though at first unavailing, when Nasser moved to create the United Arab Republic. Efforts by Persia's political system to absorb Bahrain have long been opposed by the predominantly Arab social system of Bahrain. Efforts by Iraq's political system to extend itself over Kuwait—lately become a sovereign nation through separation from the British political system—are likewise opposed by Kuwait. These are instances of state nationalisms opposing each other. What will happen when Arab state nationalisms must finally be weighed against an embracing Arab nationalism remains to be seen.

Apart from Turkey and Persia, the Middle East consists of what are generally regarded—and which generally regard themselves—as "Arab" countries. Granted that the designation is not precise, the fact remains that "Arab nationalism" does exist as a force that cannot be omitted from any empirical study of the Middle East. The boundary of an Arab social system as distinguished from other social systems cannot be drawn on the basis of any single criterion—ethnic, linguistic, cultural, or other—and probably would not be drawn in the same way by any two observers. But a precise boundary is not essential for our purpose; the evidence must speak for itself.

"The Arabs are a natural group in the world," wrote the Arab scholar Ibn Khaldun in 1377.* His own definition of an "Arab" or of a "natural group" was not made completely clear, but long before he wrote and ever since, the sense of "being Arab" has been a dominant factor in the self-definition

---

* Ibn Khaldun, *The Maggaddimah: An Introduction to History*, trans. Franz Rosenthal. Bollingen Series XLIII, Vol. I, New York: Pantheon Books, 1958, p. 250.

of many millions of people. Precisely what an "Arab" is may puzzle ethnologists, but it has never puzzled the Arabs themselves. The sense of belonging to this great social system has come down through the ages despite internal discords and violent conflicts, and still exists as a unifying force. Most conspicuous among the elements of consensus has been the common devotion to Islam—itself a product of Arab culture. Islam has had political as well as spiritual content, and led to the conquest of an empire as well as giving order to a vast intellectual outpouring of literature, art, and science.

From such an historical background it is not at all surprising that a sense of Arab nationalism impelled great numbers of Arabs to seek their own political system when World War I extinguished the Ottoman political system under which most Arabs had lain for centuries. It was in that hope that the Arabs revolted and voluntarily placed themselves under British leadership to vanquish the Turks. To accept British leadership was a practical necessity because warfare had become too technical for Arab resources alone; and Arab leadership was too decentralized for combined military operations. The diffusion of Arab nationalism through a society distributed over many thousands of miles without effective means of communication had led to local leaderships competing for sanction powers, rather than to coalition under a single Arab leader.

What actually happened after World War I is a matter of familiar history. The Allies, primarily to check the threat of a rising Arab power, fragmented the Arab Middle East by creating mandates over Iraq, Transjordan, Palestine, Syria, and Lebanon—the first three under British and the last two under French political control. During the next two or three decades the Arabs rebelled against their British and French overlords; and, ironically, the circumstances that made this movement successful was the very fragmentation designed by the Allies to avert such an event.

Successful rebellion against an established overload requires a consensus concerning leadership and authority which was difficult to produce among the widely scattered Arabs, but which came about successively within the limited areas of the separate newly-formed states. Locally, popular rebelliousness could be focused upon specific issues, and a single strong leader could be invested with the power of command. But the very way in which the new Arab states gained their liberation —at different times and under different leaderships—constrained them to remain identified with the particular land-boundaries within which their respective rebellions had been confined. Thus, for the purpose of liberation, state nationalisms achieved what Arab nationalism could not.

But this is not all. The political integration that a diffuse Arab nationalism failed to produce—in the face of group tensions and conflicts between rival leaders—now could be brought about by agreement among a few heads of state. Examples of this have already been given. The failure of early experiments to produce enduring unions shows only that political authority was extended more rapidly in those cases than consensus was developed to support it. It is possible that looser federations to begin with, based upon such consensus as existed in each case at the time, might progressively have become a more complete union as an increasing number of groups reached consensus concerning both their separate and their joint rights and sanctions. This may yet occur. History is patient and will wait out the mistakes of impatient leaders.

Up to now our examination of political change has been concerned mainly with factors which have significance in establishing the source of authority both within groups organized around particular rights and within the collectivity of such groups that comprises a nation. But a whole new set of problems arises when we look at the ways in which authority is exercised through the political system—that is, at the mechanisms of government. Our look here will be brief, because generalizations cannot carry us far. The number of variables involved in real situations is too great.

Since a nation is delimited, politically, by the extent of a single embracing authority over the sanctions exercised within it, continuity of law and order requires that conflicts within the structure of group leaderships be resolved in such a way that one ascending system of authority will be capable of exercising effective sanctions despite any internal opposition to it. It will be recalled that when a group organizes itself into a social system interacting in response to some common belief in a right, it grants sanction authority based upon consensus. Why such authority is granted to one person instead of to another is a question to which we do not have the answer, but in any given case we may presume that consensus authority is given to the leader who is regarded by that consensus as being best qualified to safeguard the group right. This applies equally as groups and their leaders are assimilated to more embracing groups, thus producing the hierarchy of leaderships which leads to the supreme national authority.

The question arises, what does a national leader require in order to go on being a national leader? What tests must he meet? For one thing, he must maintain consensus support of the people—or provide a power substitute for it. In a new nation his first test is to establish and maintain sovereignty by successfully opposing all efforts to impose external authority. As long as this is an active threat, popular consensus is almost assured: the national leader has nationalism on his side. But, sovereignty attained, consensus rests upon the balance among an indefinite number of diverse and often

conflicting new popular goals which produce new groups
with rival leaders, and contests between new and traditional
groups. When this comes about, most Middle East leaders
have seized the instruments of power that had been first
accorded them by consensus, and have used them to win whatever other power they needed to exercise authority by command—at least for a time. We can look at evidence on this
point.

Among the earliest cases, of contemporary interest, is that
of the late Ibn Saud. He established sovereignty in a residual
tribal society left over from the division of the mandates following World War I. He won consensus acceptance which
remained strong for many years, in part no doubt because of
his exceptional personal characteristics—which represent the
social scientists' concept of *charisma*—but even more by exploiting his traditional status as head of the Wahabi religious
sect with its strong consensus in his support. But Ibn Saud
left nothing to chance; the reactionary religious *ulema* did
not always approve his conduct, and he had hereditary rivals
among the tribes. While his early power was high he used it
to provide a chain of radio stations over his widespread domain, and through them he expediently directed a mobile
force of picked men with machine-guns mounted in trucks.
With these resources at his disposal he acquired the additional power he needed, including sole rights to later oil
royalties. Thus the first necessity for a successful political
system was provided—mechanisms for its own survival.

Ataturk took an opposite course in respect to traditional
consensus by eliminating it lock, stock, and barrel, and won
an even stronger *non*traditional consensus by introducing
innovations at a rate which kept his eager followers panting
to stay abreast of them. But he also provided more dependable mechanisms of political survival—and used them ruth-
lessly more than once. These included progressively nearly

all the power devices of a modern Western government, at least in skeleton form, in addition to some no longer approved in the West.

Reza Shah in Persia tried a short-cut toward the same end without either eliminating the sources of conflicting traditional consensus—little of which supported him—or introducing the kinds of innovations that served to engender a new consensus in his favor. His seizure of power, and his use of it, were complete for a time but became useless when he failed to preserve national sovereignty, lost through Allied occupation. His sucessor, Mohammed Reza, when sovereignty was re-established, sought to regain the traditional consensus acceptance of kingship, but lacked the perspicuity which led to King Farouk's doleful observation shortly before his downfall in Egypt, that soon there would be only five kings left in the world—the kings of hearts, spades, diamonds, and clubs, and the King of England.

As Shah Mohammed Reza learned more about political evolution—particularly under Mossadegh's somewhat rude tutelage—he made great efforts to win the leadership of new nontraditional groups and the consensus support that goes with that leadership. But Persia has never been the homeland of consensus except within closely knit groups—the low level of mobilization is one reason, cultural and social heterogeneity another. Mohammed Reza's consensus support rallied with his First Seven-Year Plan. This might also have been a very effective survival mechanism for a new political system, had it succeeded; but when it failed because of the suspension of oil revenues in 1951 an overwhelming—if localized—consensus favored Mossadegh. Traditional and nontraditional groups and leaderships in Persia since World War I have remained too nearly balanced to produce any important political development since that time.

The evidence sketched here warrants the conclusion—as

far as this evidence goes—that the survival factor is an important one in determining what a government does, and what governing mechanisms will first be provided. Evidently, too, the importance is a real one—not many new political systems in the Middle East have survived long enough to accomplish whatever other goals they had—or if they have survived they have lacked the mechanisms necessary for other achievements. What are these achievement mechanisms?

Most national leaders have recognized that achievement of popular goals is a long-run requirement for survival, and promises of such achievements have been a conspicuous device for winning consensus support. But in nearly every case —Ataturk is a notable exception—national leaders have failed to recognize the *means* through which popular goals could be reached. What was said in an earlier chapter about means values need not be repeated—but it has high relevance here. Struggling, illiterate masses newly awakened to the possibilities of a better life may know what they want, but they cannot be expected to know what it takes to get it. This is why they need leaders, and subconsciously—perhaps—why they are willing to follow those leaders.

Leaders recognize the popular goal of independence sought through nationalism; but once achieved, this goal may shut off more avenues toward further goals than it opens. Nationalism itself is an urge only toward gaining the right to say what the new fashion of life will be—not either an urge or a guide toward what is necessary to bring that way about.

The first achievement mechanism a new government needs is not a five-year or seven-year plan for steel mills, hydroelectric complexes, and monumental public buildings— but five-year or seven-year plans for creating new values and new capabilities in the people themselves. The potential for national growth thus generated could not be vaingloriously proclaimed in terms of kilowatt-hours, but it would be worth much more to the country than the achievements that have been thus reported by both Middle East governments and foreign-aid agencies. The mechanism required here is capable administrative organization in such fields as education (primary, secondary, adult, agricultural, and other vocational fields), public health, and social welfare generally—including not only material well-being but the adjustment to new ways of life. In short, governments should have the means of finding the answers to the kinds of questions that have been raised in the preceding chapter and in this one. The fact is that most Middle East leaders do *not* know what their people want or how to enable them to get it. Western policy-makers must find answers to these questions. Otherwise Middle East governments will continue to fall. The people are impatient, and there is no shortage of ambitious new leaders.

Chapter Eight

A Panorama of National Growth

FOR GENERATIONS prior to World War I the Middle East slept. Neither its own occasional uneasy turnings nor localized Western exploitation—political, strategic, or commercial —produced significant changes in the people or in their institutions. But the single generation since World War I saw the entire region in upheaval. Change was everywhere, and was of many kinds—cultural, social, political, economic, and technological. And today the Middle East is still in ferment.

The policy-maker is deeply concerned with the ways in which these changes have come about. But continual change, not only in a particular situation with which he may be dealing but in the surroundings which give it a setting, makes it impossible for him to organize and analyze his data in relation to any static frame of reference—as he might do if his problem were one of geological or hydrographic investigation, or of history long past. The policy-maker's problem is typically one of change—how to change the way in which change is taking place. He depends heavily upon experience, but yesterday's experience may not be valid today unless the relationship it disclosed between variables continues to exist over a considerable range of change. But relationships between *which* variables, and over *what* range of change before the experience loses validity?

What does our experience in Middle East countries tell us? Almost every kind of aid that we have given to any Middle East country and almost every general position that we have taken within that region has worked well in some cases and proved a failure in others. This has been true also of measures taken by the people and governments of the Middle East countries themselves in their own efforts toward advancement. Our technical and economic aid to Turkey in the early 1950's was a boon to that country and unquestionably served our own national security and other interests. But in Saudi Arabia, at about the same time, our aid program, which had the same general intentions as the one in Turkey, proved a dismal failure and ended in a humiliating cancellation by the King. And our continued support of the Turkish government's program in the late 1950's probably hastened that government's collapse. Our refusal to support the Shah of Persia between 1948 and 1951 made his downfall almost certain. The support we have given him since the late 1950's may have strengthened popular opposition to his government more than it has strengthened him. Middle East dictators have been both good and bad—by our standards of performance if not of principle. Some educational systems that we have helped— particularly at advanced levels—have produced more rebels than law-makers and technologists. And so it goes. To construct a reference frame which retains reasonable validity under change is not easy from such varied experience, and may not be possible. But unless it is possible the prospect for learning from experience is cheerless.

In a small way, but at least one which sharpens the hard edges of reality, my own experience has made me aware of the problems faced by policy-makers. As a consultant to both private and government clients I have been obliged to interpret what I have seen in terms that would contribute helpfully to the clients' decisions. Their problems have varied widely. In a given situation, what factors determine the security of foreign capital invested within the country, and how should those factors be evaluated? Should "head office" functions be established within a particular Middle East country, or be maintained in London or New York? To what extent should investment, or management, be shared with local people? To what extent should a private foreign company take part in political activities, devising new legislation, establishing educational facilities, or the promotion of public health and other social welfare programs? And more generally, what factors affect the balancing of "interests" of a foreign company and a national government—interests of many kinds, separate, joint, mutual, common, conflicting? What sanctions can be applied by each party to safeguard its interests, and what countersanctions by the other? Superficially, such problems might seem quite different from those confronting a maker of public policy. But the factors disclosed at the first level of analysis are largely common to both. And the deeper we look the more identical they become.

I had one advantage over many of our public policy-makers; I was free from most of the restraints that bound them—to particular countries, to short tours of duty, to conventional approaches, to conflicting commitments, to compromise judgments which would leave no one out on a limb. I shared one advantage with them; we could all identify parts of most problems as involving, essentially, certain factors which had already been studied systematically and could be dealt with by appropriate specialists—economists, public health experts, lawyers, engineers, agriculturists. I also shared one disadvantage with them; we were alike in having no organized source of guidance in the one field that produced most of our problems—the field of social behavior. Here we all were thrown back on what could be observed and what could be made out of it. Lacking investigative techniques based upon specialized knowledge, we had to devise pragmatic ones of our own.

One requirement seemed to be to find some order in the moving panorama presented by the Middle East over the last forty years during which most changes of contemporary interest have taken place. This approach might lead to a reference frame within which seemingly inconsistent evidence of change would be found consistent *when placed in its proper setting;* and such a frame would permit a synthesis of observations of different kinds and at different times into a meaningful over-all view.

In the Middle East we can look at fifteen or more cases of national growth (counting nine nations and the principal shaikhdoms or groups of shaikhdoms) with strong common characteristics among them as well as wide differences, and see almost the entire range of advancement from traditional tribal communities to instances of relatively high modernity. Surely, if order exists in the way national growth takes place, it should be found here.

In the early 1920's these countries had advanced to different levels but they were generally characterized by their small privileged elites, illiterate, poverty-stricken masses, and traditionally despotic governments, some of which were under foreign control. The differences among the countries were largely explainable by familiar historical factors. By 1960 most of the countries had changed vastly, and furthermore the range of difference among them was greater. They can be arrayed on the basis of the level reached in 1960 relative to Western standards. A precise ranking on this basis would depend upon definitions of criteria and methods of measuring; but it is unlikely that refinements would greatly change the listing. Turkey and Egypt would be near the top; Saudi Arabia, Yemen, and the lesser coastal shaikhdoms near the bottom; and Lebanon, Syria, Persia, Bahrain, Kuwait, Iraq, and Jordan strung along between.

For a first appraisal this array can be placed in a more familiar context by noting that its top barely reaches the bottom rung of a corresponding array of modern Western countries. Again, refined comparative measurements are not necessary; various references make this clear. For example, Rostow's "five stages" of development—*traditional society, preconditions for take-off, take-off, drive toward maturity,* and *high mass consumption*—can be applied to both the Middle East and the West.* Rostow rates Turkey alone among Middle East countries as having reached the stage of *take-off,* which is the starting point of Western economic institutions. And students of Turkish affairs are likely to question even this.

Another reference is furnished by John Kenneth Galbraith and his five "critical requirements" for national advancement, all of which, he says, must be present for growth to be sustained.† These are: (1) general literacy, and a substantial educated elite; (2) a substantial measure of social justice; (3) reliable apparatus of government and public administration; (4) clear and purposeful developmental objectives; and (5) capital and technology. All are present in modern Western societies. Few Middle East countries meet any of these requirements—none meets them all.

In the Middle East array indicated here, relative rank is based upon directly observable evidence. Examples are class

---

* W. W. Rostow, *The Process of Economic Growth.* New York: W. W. Norton, 1962, pp. 307 ff.
† J. K. Galbraith, "A Positive Approach to Economic Aid," *Foreign Affairs,* April 1961, pp. 444 ff.

distinctions and discriminations; structure and activities of governments; states of education, health, and housing; kinds of occupations; consumption habits; means of communication; and variously manifested evidences of entrepreneurship (defined broadly as economic activity aimed at producing or contributing to a surplus over subsistence requirements).

In general, the higher a country in the array, the more the kinds of change that can be observed since World War I, and also the greater the degree of change of any particular kind. For example, progressively toward the top of the array there is increasing diversity of such broad categories of change as cultural, social, political, and economic; but the latter two have almost no relevance for those countries near the bottom of the array. And although some cultural and social changes can be observed throughout, the status of women, for example, has changed far more in Turkey, where in many ways women are on an equal footing with men, than in countries progressively lower in the scale.

Actually, in our seach for regularity in the growth process, what we observe directly is not *kinds* of change, but specific instances of behavior or condition. A difference between what is observed at two points in time indicates change; but the number and the diversity of such specific instances of change are so great that no common order can be discerned. Each change was the product of a combination of variables that is not likely to be repeated. The proximate cause in a given instance may have been the appearance of a strong leader, for example, or war, foreign intervention, or the discovery of oil. Circumstances accidental to a given case obscure fundamental regularities in the growth process.

The first step toward finding order in empirically observed data—a standard one in the scientific method—is to classify what has been observed into kinds that appear to act in the same way in respect to the problem under study.

However, even kinds of change have come about for very different proximate reasons in the different countries, just as was said of specific instances of change. In respect to cause, order is masked by accident even among kinds of change.

But if instead of looking for causes we look at the sequence in which various kinds of change have occurred throughout the Middle East, there is a possibility that some order can be found. At least we can proceed in the belief that this may be so, and examine the evidence with this in mind.

The sum total of Middle East observations is far too huge a haystack to search for a needle that may or may not exist, but we can make a first approach by selecting certain evidence which appears to be closely related to growth and which, if divested of extraneous detail, should reflect sequence in kinds of change if such sequence exists. Since it is *national* growth that concerns us, each country must be examined for indications of change. If this leads to a composite picture which represents without substantial distortion what is found in the separate cases, we may be able to reach a conclusion relating sequence of change to national growth.

Since what concerns us is regularity among kinds of change, we must select observed instances of change that represent kinds common to as many countries as possible. The mobilization of a people for social action, discussed earlier, is one such change. But mobilization is only a preparation for social action. A more generative change comes when a preponderant mass of a society awakens to the realization that much of the world is better off than they are—freer from privation and oppression—and that relief from their state is not only possible but worth striving for. This kind of change, a massive increase of popular motivation for satisfying new desires, can be noted in many Middle East countries during the last generation, and in some countries more than once. Other frequently noted kinds of change have been the

emergence of new popular leaders (not identified with traditional groups); the overthrow of one ruling regime and its
replacement by another; the appearance of new forms of government departing from traditional patterns; social-system
changes resulting from a diversity of innovations—technological, economic, ideological—that tend to make old institutions obsolete and new ones necessary; and technological and
economic changes that are in themselves so far-reaching in
effect as to warrant a separate classification that includes
mechanized agriculture, expanding industries, new banking
systems, and the like.

If specific instances of such kinds of change are set down
as observed in each country, with their approximate dates in
each case, our simplified panorama begins to take form. Their
frequency distribution on a time scale since World War I
will show different kinds of change, salient to national growth,
tending to form clusters in different periods. In some periods,
to be sure, more than one kind of change will tend to concentrate; and some kinds of change may either disappear or
persist into later periods.

This historical panorama can be visualized with the aid of
a diagram. In *Fig. I* the horizontal scale shows time, starting
with World War I. No vertical scale can be shown, because
few of the variables that enter into the different kinds of
change depicted can be quantified—and even if they could
be, no single unit would be common to them all. For equally
obvious reasons it is impracticable, at least within the scope
of this study, to plot the actual number of observed instances
of change, since these varied widely in nature and significance.
But the diagram does suggest, by the prominence of each
shaded area, the *kind* of change that was preponderant at
different times.

Thus in Turkey, where the society became highly mobilized during Ataturk's rule, three times during the total period

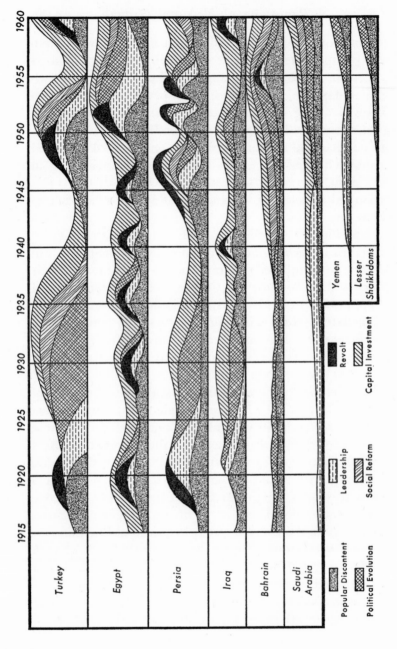

Fig. I

covered the prevailing popular attitude has changed from one of passivity or relative contentment to one of high discontent and renewed motivation for change. These periods are indicated by three pronounced "bulges" in the "popular discontent" band: namely, the World War I period (including the Turco-Greek War ending in 1922); the period from Ataturk's death in 1938 to shortly after the change in government in 1950; and again from around 1955 until the overthrow of the Menderes government in 1959. Between those bulges popular discontent—or at least positively manifested desire for change—dropped to almost nothing until, for some reason, it began noticeably to rise again.

As for the specific instances that produced these three surges in popular discontent, it is hardly necessary for our present purposes to do more than recall that the first period marks the passing of "the sick man of Europe," ending an era of corrupt and despotic rule under the Ottoman dynasty that can scarcely be matched in modern history. Popular discontent in those circumstances can hardly be questioned. The two later periods could be documented by referring to the press of those times and noting such manifestations as the frequent suppressions of the press itself, the use of troops to quell riots, the withdrawal of private funds from productive investments, a flourishing "black market," bans on public meetings, confiscatory taxes and consequent evasive tactics, shortages of food and other consumer necessities, government-controlled elections, and increasingly audible remonstrations by the people against those and other oppressions and privations.

If we look next at Persia, evidence of high popular discontent shows five clusters or periods of concentration. The first one, declining in the middle 1920's, marked the closing years of the Qajar dynasty, presided over at that time by a despotic Shah and a pusillanimous Parliament. Much the same could be said of this period as was said of the corresponding period in Turkey. Popular discontent rose for the second time after the close of World War II. The rapacious elite oligarchy that had seized effective control of the country after Reza Shah's abdication in 1941 bled both the treasury and the current production of the country into their own or their landlord henchmen's pockets. Tribes and urban populations became openly defiant against the central government; and the peasant population, facing starvation and pestilence, displayed increasing sullenness and resentment. Azerbaijan was in open revolt. The "press"—scarcely to be dignified by the term—was nothing more than paid organs for slander, available to the highest bidder. The third cluster of symptoms of popular discontent reached its height in 1950–1951 with the failure of the first Seven-Year Plan. Its marks were unmistakable: street riots, assassinations, clashes with army and police, clamors for reforms in government, unconcealed hostility toward the British, and much more. Mobilization, though limited to the cities, was beginning to engender mass social action. The fourth peak in 1953 differed little from the third and might be regarded as a renewal of it following a brief period of vain hope and expectation. The fifth period is still waxing strong as of this writing. When it will reach its peak is for the future to tell, but increasing mobilization is bringing that time nearer.

In Iraq there were three periods of high popular discontent. The first one, at its maximum around 1921, reflected the frustrated hopes of the Arab population to win their freedom —after long years of Ottoman rule—as a result of their revolt and assistance to the victorious Allies in World War I. The second period was a long one, made complex both by the abundance and the forcible suppression of its manifestations. It rose and fell during almost the entire period from the death of King Faisal I in 1933 to the overthrow of the

Hashemite dynasty in 1959. During this quarter-century, standard chronologies of Iraqi affairs show something like forty-five separate "revolts" against the government in different parts of the country—an average approaching one every six months, although in fact concentrated at certain times more than at others. The 1941 rebellion of Raschid Ali Al Gaillani actually resulted in his seizing control of the government for a brief time. Popular resentment could be largely explained by the lack of improvement in the conditions of life of three-fourths of the population. Its manifestations were chiefly uprisings against those who were considered responsible—the Hashemite dynasty, landlord and other privileged elites, and the British. The third period of concentrated symptoms of discontent is still prominently evidenced in the early 1960's, although there were signs that its peak perhaps coincided with the overthrow of the Hashemite dynasty in 1959. It is somewhat set apart from the long second period by a few years of relative quite following World War II. The sporadic nature of the rebellious outbreaks reflects the low social mobilization of the society.

The long second period of discontent in Iraq is paralleled by corresponding periods in the other Middle East countries in which a foreign power, British or French, either ruled outright or dominated the national government. Such cases include Egypt, Iraq, and Bahrain among the countries shown in *Fig. I,* and Syria, Lebanon, Jordan, and Kuwait among those not shown on the chart. In all those cases popular resentment against the exercise of foreign authority within the country was added to discontent from other sources.

We can now add evidence of other kinds of change and represent them by different bands on the same chart. The band that represents popular leadership indicates those times when this factor was significant in determining the affairs of the country. The distinguishing quality of leadership, for

our purposes here, is that it signifies the readiness of followers to be led, rather than the capability of a leader to compel,
a highly important distinction. The instances shown on the
chart include the following:

In Turkey, Ataturk in 1920, Menderes in 1946, and—less
conspicuously—Gursal in 1959.

In Egypt, Nasser in 1952 (shared with Naguib for a short
time).

In Persia, Reza Shah in 1921, Mohammed Reza Pahlavi
in 1946, Mossadegh in 1950, and Mohammed Reza Pahlavi
again, briefly, in 1953.

In Iraq, King Faisal himself during the latter years of his
reign, Raschid Ali Al Gaillani briefly around 1940, and
Kassem in 1959.

In Bahrain, Abdurrahman Al Bekhir in 1954.

Although not shown in the chart, Kuwatly in Syria and
Al Khuri in Lebanon, both in 1941, can be included.

All these leaders apparently were regarded as liberators by
large masses of people who placed themselves willingly under
their command. At least it can be observed that in most cases
these leaders exercised command without visible use of power
to enforce it, although in all cases except those of Mossadegh,
Al Gaillani, and Al Bekhir such power was in the leaders'
hands. In each of these instances of conspicuous leadership
there were also lesser leaders, some attached to the dominant
one and others in opposition to him and frequently to one
another. What is important is that during certain periods in
each country, the most conspicuous evidence of change is
that of popular leaders contesting for popular support.

Periods of successful revolt against the government in
power are represented by the black band on the chart. The
evidence of these instances is so clear that no detailing is necessary here. It should be noted, however, that "revolt" took
various forms, depending upon what was required in each

instance to replace one ruling regime with another. Thus the Ottoman and Qajar regimes, in Turkey and Persia respectively, were moribund and crumbled under the pressures of the times; Ataturk and Reza Shah simply took over. The revolt in Turkey in 1950 was expressed by popular ballot in a truly free election—probably the sole instance of its kind in Middle East history. It was made possible in this case by Inonu's decision to permit a free election, because the flagrantly rigged election of 1946 resulted in a sinister threat of open rebellion. Mohammed Reza's regime in Persia was overthrown in 1951 by the defection of most who had supported it and their voluntary attachment to the opposition movement headed by Mossadegh. In other instances overthrow was brought about by the military—in Iraq (1959) with savage violence, but in most cases without bloodshed, and probably because the army was the only organization in the country responsive to popular consensus and also capable of coordinated action. Syria and Lebanon were emancipated from Vichy French domination largely by negotiation with the Western Allies during World War II; and Syria separated herself from the United Arab Republic (controlled by Nasser) by proclamation in 1961.

Periods in which there was active political evolution are also shown, chiefly evidenced by the spectacle of popular leaders seizing or devising instruments through which authority can be exercised by power; or by the development of new mechanisms within an established government. Specific instances of this kind of change vary widely in nature, depending upon the mechanisms already existing and the aims of those in power.

Thus in Turkey the creation of a new structure of national government began with the re-establishment of Turkish sovereignty, all but lost in World War I, through the Lausanne Treaty of 1923. Turkey was proclaimed a republic later that same year, and in the following year an organic law was decreed—later to become a constitution—in which the principles that were to govern the republic were set out. This was Ataturk's work, increasingly shared by able men. The elaboration of this new government was the most conspicuous occurrence in Turkish history during the decade 1924–1934, by the end of which most of the administrative mechanisms through which the country was to be governed for the following twenty-five years had at least been conceived and their functions defined. As later evidence shows, not everything worked perfectly, particularly after Ataturk's death. Evidences of reorganization in government are massed again around 1950, and once more in 1960.

Evidences of political evolution form several clusters in the case of Persia. The first corresponds in time and to a certain extent in character with the first one in Turkey, although Reza Shah's efforts fell far short of Ataturk's in results— partly because he had less to build on. It is shown in *Fig. I* as reaching a peak around 1930. The next changes of this kind are observed around 1947–1948, reflecting Shah Mohammed Reza Pahlavi's efforts at political and administrative reform —more efforts than results, although high principles of government were proclaimed. The constitution (of 1906) was at least brought back into view, a senate created, and various reform bills enacted—pre-eminent among which was the bill establishing the Seven-Year Plan. Again in 1951–1953 Mossadegh strove to reform the government, but his program was short-lived.

In Iraq the same kind of change—reorganization of government by a new source of authority as a mechanism for the exercise of that authority—is evidenced first in quite a different way from that observed in Turkey and Persia. The change in Iraq was produced by foreign rather than by national authority. But it has the same category in our picture. The earliest evidence shows a foreign power, Britain, establishing a government under the Mandate of 1920, converted at least nominally in 1921 into a monarchy in treaty alliance with the British. As might be expected, the government installed by the British was an effective one from the start, at least from the British point of view; and although evidences of its development continued as the Iraqis themselves became increasingly capable of self-rule, no concentrations of political evolution are noted again until 1948. At that time it was signaled prominently by the rejection of the Portsmouth Treaty, negotiated abortively by Nuri Pasha and Saleh Jabr, the prime minister of the moment. This treaty, if consummated, would have continued the historical realtionship between Iraq and Great Britain—by then regarded as servitude by most Iraqis—and its rejection by the chamber of deputies coincided with and to some extent stimulated a new effort to create a truly independent Iraqi government—nationalism at work. Evidences of this effort continued for several years—reinvigorated ministries, more attention to social reforms, increased strength of "loyal opposition" political parties, more realistic planning for development—but the "pro-British" government of Nuri Pasha proved sufficiently elastic to absorb those efforts toward change without substantial modification in its workings. The next cluster of evidence marking political evolution does not appear until after the coup of 1959—nationalism triumphant.

In Egypt little significant political evolution is noted until the coup of 1952. Nominal power had been transferred from British to Egyptian hands by 1936 but was subordinated to a series of treaties and protocols which left the British in effective control. Internally, the period was marked only by rival party clashes and futile efforts to shake off British domination.

In Syria, not represented in *Fig. I,* the political situation since the republic was established has remained too volatile to provide evidence of orderly political development. In Lebanon somewhat the same may be said, although the ruling oligarchy has proved to be more durable—or perhaps simply less subject to stress because popular discontent was less.

Evidences of significant change in the social structure and prevailing ways of life of the people are concentrated mainly in the periods shown in another band on the diagram. In Turkey, such evidence is most conspicuous in 1925–1935, before *étatisme* took full hold in the government, and 1950–1955 under Menderes. In Persia there has been little such evidence at any time. In Iraq, too, except in the centers of principal British activity, little change in social conditions can be seen, although some evidence appears in the early 1950's. Nor is there much evidence of marked change in the conditions of life among the masses of people in Egypt, Syria, Lebanon, or Jordan during the period covered. In Bahrain social change can be seen continuously from the early 1930's onward; and in Saudi Arabia, from the early 1950's.

Evidences of substantial capital investment in Turkey were concentrated in two main periods, the 1930's and the 1950's. In Persia there were also two main periods of national investment, the 1930's and the years after 1955, although oil-company investment in the oil region was more or less continuous from 1914 on. In Iraq relatively heavy capital investments, mostly in public works in which British interests were involved, began almost immediately after the national government was formed in 1921, and continued with only minor fluctuations until the rebellion of 1959. A similar steady program of capital investment, also chiefly in public works—apart from the oil company's own investment—can be seen in Bahrain from the middle 1930's to the present time. In Egypt relatively heavy capital investments have been made for many years—British, French, and Egyptian—in both public works and in private factories and buildings. This has also been true on a smaller scale in Lebanon, with private capital both foreign and national. Mainly during the last decade both Saudi Arabia and Kuwait have invested very large sums of public capital in public works, including schools and hospitals, although relatively little has gone into industrial undertakings except by the oil companies.

There may be an objection here that the way I have indicated periods of high capital investment is too casual to provide a basis for sound conclusions, and that at least in this case a statistical presentation could have been made. But my purpose here is not to make a technical analysis of capital investment and its effect upon national growth. My present concern is limited to the sequence in which certain kinds of change have been most conspicuous, as a general guide for recognizing the circumstances under which each kind has become crucially significant. Furthermore, capital investment in the Middle East has been of many kinds over the period covered, and its effect upon a national economy ranges equally widely. Comparisons between ratios—for example, of investment to gross national income—or between rates of investment per capita may be more misleading than instructive when the investments in the different cases have been for military installations, or for oil refineries which had little effect upon the royalties paid to the country, or for monumental public works or buildings done largely for the benefit of the contractors, or for state-owned industrial plants which operate at half capacity—if at all. My purpose is to identify the periods in which high capital investments have been made, to see whether those periods are associated with periods in which any other kinds of change have been notable.

Some tentative inferences can now be made on the basis of this review of the kinds of change that have taken place in the Middle East.

1. Until a people has become mobilized for social action, any imposed change is provisional—subject to ratification by popular consensus when mobilization occurs.

2. New popular leaders have emerged in times of widespread popular discontent—rarely at other times.

3. Periods in which a national government has been dominated by a foreign power have been low in evidence of sustained personal leadership; that is, such leadership either has been suppressed by or has eliminated that foreign domination.

4. Until popular leaders have emerged, no successful revolt against a ruling regime has occurred; that is, successful revolts have resulted from effective organization and direction, not directly from popular discontent.

5. Following all observed instances of successful revolt, a popular leader has arrogated to himself sufficient instruments of power to make his authority superior to all opposition, at least for a time, and has modified old and created new mechanisms of government to insure his political survival.

6. Periods of substantial social advancement have followed—not preceded—periods of political advancement, and have not occurred until political authority has been made secure.

7. Periods of substantial popular discontent, rebellion, political reform, or social reform appear to have been largely independent of periods of high capital investment.

8. High technological innovation and capital investment appear to play a dominant role in national growth only after political and social reforms have taken place and new basic political and social institutions established.

These tentative inferences are pictured in *Fig. II* which suggests how successive "waves" of change become critically important as their growth curves develop. Thus the "old regime" governing a traditional society is rejected when popular discontent stimulates new leaders to overthrow it and set up a political system of their own. The society itself then undergoes changes in adaptation to new goals and means of achieving them, finally arriving at a point where technology and capital investment in productive undertakings become the limiting factor on both rate and extent of growth. Each kind of change shown plays its own part in stimulating and sustaining the process of growth, and if any kind is missing,

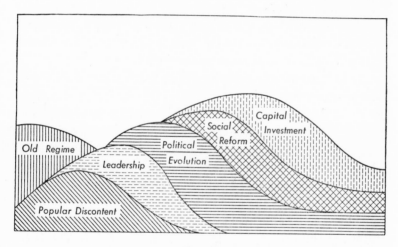

Fig. II

or takes place inadequately, the growth process stops, and unless the deficiency is remedied sooner or later reverts to where a new start can be made.

It would be idle to regard this picture as representing a "law of national growth," or to claim any logical inevitability about the sequence of changes that it suggests. This is not the intention. If this simplified organization of observed events helps to place experience in significant context it will assist both in evaluating the experience as a factor in past growth and in using it for prediction.

For example, in Turkey during the few years following 1947 both engineers and economists urged the construction of a widespread system of primary, secondary, and tertiary roads. Analysis based upon accepted principles foretold with fair accuracy how this would change the pattern of food and fiber crop production, consumption, and export; also its effect on the price structure, national income, balance of payments, migration of labor, and many other things, which on the whole proved true. But in Persia in the middle 1920's engineers and economists had told Reza Shah the same things, or nearly the same. His road program included a network in Azerbaijan, potentially the greatest source of food in the country, with connections to Russia, Turkey, Iraq, and central Persia. This system was never used to any significant extent, nor was it maintained. In the middle 1940's I traveled much of it by jeep—half the time on detours around washed-out sections. Even the large expanses of new land served by those roads, which had been planted in tobacco and cotton by the State, were neglected and within a few years went back to weeds. Obviously, in the Azerbaijan case many other kinds of change had to take place before the people had either the desire or the capability to produce a surplus over traditional needs, or the means to purchase goods brought in, or a wish to travel more widely. In Chapter Six we examined motivation for change at this level and drew some inferences as to how certain motivations could be created or directed. Almost none of those things had been done in Persia, nor was the government of that time disposed to do them. On the other hand, in Turkey by 1950 there was an intense and widespread urge among the people to satisfy new desires, and a determination on the government's part to make this possible. In this combination of circumstances local private capital came out of hiding and foreign private capital moved in. Good roads facilitated the resulting spurt in growth but they did not cause it; the causes had deeper sources.

The most baffling evidence to evaluate is the part played by capital and advanced technology, which for present purposes can be taken together because in practice one usually involves the other. Certainly at some point they become crucial to growth—although little evidence of this can be found in the Middle East during the period examined here. On the basis of Middle East evidence alone we are more likely to conclude that until a traditional society has reached some relatively high level of social and political maturity, a heavy infusion of capital and technology will tend to accelerate *any* kind of change that is underway—whether for better or worse from the viewpoint of sustained national growth. This would seem a reasonable expectation. When capital is relatively plentiful, means of achievement are more available. Personal stakes are higher, conflicting interests more intense, decisions more consequential—all of which tends to raise the pressure under which interactions of all kinds take place. Examples are abundant.

In Bahrain, under Belgrave's guidance social reforms had made notable progress before substantial oil revenues became available; this progress was accelerated, rather than changed in kind, by increased investment. In Saudi Arabia we must certainly question the extent to which the great changes noted there can be attributed to "capital investment" with the connotations usually attached to that term by economists. This view is supported by the fact that oil-industry capital on a comparable scale was poured into both Iraq and Persia over an even longer period, but produced almost no social change—except a dangerous rise in tensions. The significant change that took place in Saudi Arabia at that time was the change that took place in men's minds—not in oil-refining capacity or in the elaboration of princely palaces.

References have already been made to the havoc resulting from both Ataturk's and Reza Shah's vast industrialization programs, and to that of Menderes in the late 1950's. In these cases new economic and social dislocations were produced by the investment programs; the gap between the "ins" and the "outs," the "haves" and the "have nots," became wider and the tensions greater. Something of the same can be said of the so-called "development program" of monumental public works in Iraq between 1930 and 1950. The great flood-control works were of advantage chiefly to those who had the contracts to build them. One good way to avoid flood damage is to stay out of the way of floods. A much smaller capital outlay for irrigation works that would have enabled Iraq's sparse population to increase crop production in great areas not subject to flood would have minimized the migration of starving peasants and tribesmen to the city fringes where the flood dangers were highest. Ultimately the time will come in Iraq when the ways of its two great rivers must be changed. But the time is already here—and long past—for a change in the ways of its people, and in the ways in which they are governed.

This panorama of change in the Middle East does not enable us to predict the future—the variables are far too many even if we knew what all of them were. But it does help us to understand the past and to interpret experience more reliably. We can put historical events in their proper context, and in the case of any new situation that arises, we can use past experience to interpret and understand the factors that enter crucially into the change that is taking place.

Chapter Nine

A Basis for American Policy

"THE UNITED STATES," according to the Eisenhower Doctrine, "regards as vital to the national interest and to world peace the preservation of the independence and integrity of the nations of the Middle East. To this end, if the President determines the necessity thereof, the United States is prepared to use armed forces to assist any such nation or group of nations requesting assistance against armed aggression from any country controlled by international communism. . . ." *

In 1957 when Dwight D. Eisenhower announced to the world his "policy" concerning the Middle East, most Americans accepted it as a simple if somewhat ambiguous expression of our readiness to support the people of that region against Communist aggression. But Americans were not prepared for the widespread opposition that the Eisenhower Doctrine soon met in most of the Arab states. Its prompt acceptance by Iraq—already a member of the Baghdad Pact—was a foregone conclusion, but this acceptance was repudiated

---

* H. J. Resolution 117, 85th Congress, in *Department of State Bulletin,* March 25, 1957, p. 481.

by Kassem when he took power in 1959. The pro-American regime in Lebanon also accepted the Doctrine. But even Saudi Arabia, after a first unenthusiastic show of approval in principle, quickly joined Egypt, Syria, and Jordan in a resolution "never to allow their countries to become a sphere of influence for any foreign power." * Particularly in these latter three countries the Eisenhower Doctrine was represented by Arab leaders as an American effort to place the next war's battlefields in the Middle East instead of nearer home, to replace British with American "imperialism," to seduce Middle East governments into bartering sovereignty for American aid, and to turn the Middle East countries against Communists because Americans feared Communism as a threat to their own way of life.

Thus the Eisenhower Doctrine revealed a wide gap between American and Arab views concerning the Communist threat. *The Times* of London was surely correct in characterizing the declaration as "very late, . . . fearfully vague in parts, and largely irrelevant to the main causes of Middle Eastern upheavals, tensions, and dangers." † And subsequently in the United States itself, a publication of the Council on Foreign Relations was equally correct in saying: "The truth was that . . . the Eisenhower Doctrine had not by any means succeeded in unifying the Middle East in opposition to Soviet designs. It would be more accurate to say that it had introduced a fresh element of division among Middle Eastern countries, perpetuating and in some cases accentuating the divisions already created by the Baghdad Pact and other manifestations of Western policy in past years." ‡

The positions taken by the various countries affected by

* *Documents on American Foreign Policy, 1957,* No. 55.
† *The Times* (London), Jan. 7, 1957.
‡ Richard P. Stebbins and the research staff of the Council on Foreign Relations, *The United States in World Affairs, 1957.* New York: Harper & Brothers, 1958, p. 175.

the Doctrine were, of course, relative to their own national aims. In earlier chapters we examined some of the factors involved in the national aims of the Middle East countries and in the processes for achieving those aims. But this book is not only about the Middle East. It is also concerned with American policy and the part this policy takes in resolving conflicts between our own national aims and those of other peoples. Policy must have foundations at both ends. We must now look at its foundations in our country. So now to Washington, where "doctrines" and "pacts" originate—and where policy must be made.

The term *policy* has a complex meaning, and in different contexts one or another of those meanings may be the most significant. In the present context, where we need a precise concept of policy to assist in the conduct of our relations with other countries, the significant meaning must be derived from its function as a guide for those who make decisions relating to the achievement of designated aims. Policy, therefore, is a set of criteria which guides decision-making. This definition makes a distinction between *policy* and the complex aspirations, moral principles, and beliefs held by the American people generally, which reflect a consensus of national aims.

Our national aims, in this broad sense, are very difficult to know with assurance. Aspirations, moral principles, and beliefs range widely among groups and change with circumstances. They involve far too many variables to serve directly as a guide for operational decisions. Except in respect to particular issues about which a prevailing consensus has been explicitly expressed by ballot or otherwise, our national aims can only be sensed on the basis of tradition, historical precedent, and various evidences of public opinion.

Nevertheless, national aims may be postulated—in fact must be postulated—by policy-makers as a foundation upon which to stand. Just what aims should be postulated at any given time, and what priorities should be assigned to them, can scarcely be stated categorically by those not closely in touch with all the sources of domestic and foreign information available to policy-makers. But, since policy-making rests in part upon designated aims, an analysis of the policy-making process requires that some national aims be designated as a starting point. Here we shall assume a prevailing national consensus, accepted by policy-makers, on the following general propositions.

1. Highest priority will be given to the security of the American people against aggression by any foreign power.

2. Certain traditional principles will be observed and defended, among which are:

a) American commitments to other nations should be faithfully performed.

b) All people have the right of "self-determination," subject to non-transgression upon the rights of others.

c) War for the settlement of disputes among nations should be avoided except as a last resort.

3. The economic foundations upon which the American way of life is based will be preserved and extended by means that are consistent with the foregoing aims.

Policy itself is not a statement of these or other national aims. I emphasize again that policy has a precise function in the process through which those charged with public responsibility for the achievement of national aims exercise their authority. This function is *to guide the making of decisions* through which that responsibility is discharged.

Decisions must be made at various levels of responsibility. For example, Congress has certain authority over the appropriation of public funds for foreign aid; the Senate has certain authority over treaties, and so on. The President, as Chief Executive, has wide—but not unlimited—decision-making powers, some of which he delegates to other agencies. Each decision-making agency requires policy guidance to insure consistency of purpose and coordination of action. Normally, the function of policy-making descends with the delegation of authority. Although policy-making and decision-making are separate functions, the same person or agency may perform both functions. Thus each subordinate agency to which authority for decision-making has been delegated is subject to guidance by policy formulated at a higher level, and in turn may formulate policy by which lower decision-making agencies will be guided. In any given circumstances, therefore, policy makes decisions predictable—or at least fixes the range within which they will be kept.

Starting with foreign policy formulated by the President, as a broad statement of the criteria pertaining to decisions for which he is responsible, one can identify the main variables that must be taken into account. For present purposes, only policy that is relevant to underdeveloped countries, and particularly the Middle East countries, need be considered.

When policy is examined from this point of view it will be seen at once that even the President is by no means entirely free to establish any criteria he may choose as guides for decision-making. First of all his interpretation of the "national aims" must conform reasonably well with prevailing expectations of the American people, based largely upon tradition and precedent but also based upon the representations made by the President and his party prior to his election. Besides, there are statutory limitations upon his powers, and certain overriding authorities vested in other agencies of government. The President, in other words, is not a dictator.

There are other considerations that put limitations upon policy as a guide to decision-making. Policy is concerned with the situations that exist in other countries, and those situations are real. In particular instances, when foreign situations are compared with relevant American aims, the differences show up as hard facts—not as fantasies that can be dismissed by closing our eyes. Even in a single foreign country there can be a vast number of ways in which actual situations differ from the way we Americans believe they should be. But before any executive agency of our government can take action toward changing any of those situations, a decision must be made at the appropriate level of authority as to which situations we should undertake to change, and in what order of priority. Here policy is needed to provide the criteria by which objectives will be selected and priorities assigned. The choosing of policy objectives will be discussed in more detail presently; but some of the limitations on free choice in selecting such objectives must be mentioned here in order to show more clearly the need for policy.

For one thing, in some of the situations that are observed to be different from the way we Americans believe they should be, the people concerned, or their governments, may have ideas quite different from our own on that score. Also, certain of their ways may be fixed by religious beliefs, or be bound by tradition or cultural patterns and not be susceptible to change except over a considerable time. Moreover, simply because we believe that certain things *should* be so, does not necessarily mean that we consider it our business to *make* them so. Policy must establish criteria by which decisions will take such considerations as these into account.

There is another limitation upon the selection of our objectives. To be meaningful they must be restricted to changes in existing situations that are operationally practicable through means that are available. Therefore our policy must require, as one of the tests that its objectives must pass, that suitable means of accomplishment can also be defined. This introduces limitations based upon facts and those facts must be ascertained. Each of the means available to our government for bringing about changed situations in other countries has limitations not only upon its capability for producing changes of various kinds, but also upon its availability for such purposes. Policy must provide tests for both points—suitability as a means, and priority of allocation.

With all these considerations in mind we can say that American policy, as applying to the Middle East countries, is a statement of the tests that must be met by decisions that relate to the use of American resources of any kind, to insure that such use will have maximum effect in bringing existing situations in the Middle East into conformity with American national aims as stipulated for or postulated by the policymaker.

Since policy guides decision-making, we must see what is involved in the kinds of decisions which policy is called upon to guide. Broadly speaking, these include all the decisions that must be made in order to achieve our national aims. But policy focuses upon decisions that are based upon personal judgment backed by authority—sometimes descriptively referred to as "administrative" or "executive" decisions—not upon decisions that involve only technical principles or operational necessities.

In the context of our foreign relations, whoever makes such a decision is concerned in some way with change, and ordinarily he is trying to bring some change about. Even if he wishes to *prevent* a particular change, he must change something in order to prevent it. Sometimes, it is true, he may deliberately decide not to seek any change whatever; but, even so, before he can intelligently arrive at such a decision he must consider the desirability of possible changes and the costs of bringing them about. One is justified, then, in identifying decisions with the idea of change. Two things must be decided: first, the kind of change to be sought, and, second, the means through which such a change can be brought about. These two components of a decision will be referred to as the *policy objective* and the *operational objective,* more explicitly defined as follows:

A policy objective is a specified change in behavior, sought by the policy-maker. When a policy-maker decides for any reason to apply available resources toward changing behavior, he must define what that change is to be; that is, how future behavior is to differ from what it has been. Ordinarily this can be done most simply by describing what the terminal behavior is to be after the change has been made. Thus policy objectives might be indicated, in given cases, as inducing people: to vote in public elections (or enabling them to do so if this were not possible before); to diversify their crops, or to produce a surplus for the cash market; to send their children to school; to accept legislation enacted by the central government; to acquire and use new skills for designated purposes. On the presumption that existing behavior is different from that described, implementing the indicated change becomes a policy objective.

The policy objective is not concerned directly with the conditions surrounding the people whose behavior is to be changed—whether physical, social, political, or other. These are simply factors which affect behavior. The sole function of the policy objective is to indicate the change in behavior that is sought. But this one thing it must do explicitly.

The other component of a decision, the operational objective, is the specification of an action to be taken through the exercise of the resources which the policy-maker (or the institution he represents) directs. Ordinarily such a specification is made by designating or describing the immediate terminal result of the action: for example, a dam at a certain place, a daily broadcast of a prescribed nature, an agricultural credit bank, or a school for teachers.

Operational objectives must be described in terms that are specific to the resource through which action is taken—not in terms of the behavior that is to be changed, or the reasons for changing it. An operational objective, in other words, is a specific task assigned to an operational agency, described in terms which tell that agency precisely what it is to accomplish through the application of its own techniques.

Just as a policy objective and an operational objective, as defined, are the two components of a decision, they also represent the two central ideas that are involved in making policy. For the policymaker's function is to say *how* policy objectives are to be selected and their relative priorities determined, and *how* operational objectives are to be chosen and assigned.

Since we are focusing here on policy-making as a function in the administration of our national affairs, we can relate policy directly to the national aims which have been designated to or postulated by the policy-maker. Those premises afford one frame of reference by which the policy-maker can identify and evaluate changes that need to be brought about. On this basis we can say that the first test of a policy objective is that it must serve our own national aims. Just how this test can be applied to both selection and priority of policy objectives can be shown more clearly after other considerations have been discussed.

A second frame of reference for the identification and evaluation of policy objectives is provided by the national aims of a given Middle East country—in so far as they are known. Most of the change that the policy-maker seeks to bring about will be change in what other people do. But what those people do will be determined largely by what they want. They too want change—and probably much more than we want it for them—but it may not be the same change. If the changes that we define as our policy objectives are also changes that those people want, a common effort can be made. But if the changes sought are in conflict, so will the efforts be. In such a case we may abandon the objective, or defer it by setting an intermediate policy objective—namely, to change what the people *want*. This rests upon the sound premise that it is what people want that they will try to get. It is buttressed also by the demonstrated fact that what people want can be changed. This points up the fact that frequently a policy objective, as first defined, can be reached only step by step, through lesser objectives that are achieved progressively.

Finally, a third framework of reference for the selection and priority of policy objectives is fixed by the capabilities of available means for bringing change about. Policy, that is, is concerned with what is possible—not what is merely desirable. Unless an operational objective can be specified as a means through which a given change can be effected, the policy objective remains ephemeral. It might be said that the main function of policy objectives is to make possible the specification of effective operational objectives. Therefore a test from this point of view is demanded. Such a test may show that a policy objective as first defined may need to be broken down into parts, each with its own operational objective. And just as a policy objective without an operational objective is sterile, so is an operational objective that is not oriented by a policy objective.

But there are rigorous limitations on the capabilities of operational instruments, fixed by technical factors and not by the intentions of the policy-maker. A detailed examination of the mechanisms and techniques through which changes of various kinds can be brought about would far exceed the scope of this study. However, the importance of knowing what those capabilities and limitations are warrants at least pointing to the directions that further examination should take.

Operational objectives may be reached by employing any or all of the resources and techniques that are familiarly

classed as diplomatic, political, military, economic, technological, psychological, and cultural. Most such techniques require
peculiar skills. Given adequate resources, each is capable, generally speaking, of producing whatever end result—normal to
that technique—is designated for it. This is all that must be
asked of it. In any given situation those who have skill in the
exercise of a particular technique will be able to say what
limitations there are on what can be done, and what resources will be required.

It by no means follows, however, that specialists in these
operational techniques can evaluate the effects that the tasks
they perform will have in producing changed behavior within
another society. Whatever the work performed, it simply adds
to the system of behavioral factors that already exists in that
society. Its effect, therefore, can be predicted only to the extent that the existing system of behavioral factors is understood. Almost anything that we do in a foreign country produces side-effects, that is, consequences other than those
explicit to the work itself, which in many cases are more important than the direct end result of our action. As a matter
of fact, it is frequently those secondary consequences of an
operational objective, of which the operational agency itself
is unaware, that are most significant to the policy-maker. A
few illustrations will make this point clear.

In a private meeting with several reform-minded Iraqi
ministers in the late 1940's, I was told that most of the land
to be benefited by a large dam-building project (supported
by United States aid funds and technical advice) had been
bought up by privileged persons, at the going price for arid
land, before the details of the project became publicly known.
Judged by conventional Western technical and economic
criteria, the dam project was eminently sound; but its effect
upon an already resentful and despairing peasant population,
when they saw it only making rich men richer, was quite op-

posite from what an American policy-maker would have wanted—or what an engineer or an economist would have predicted. A somewhat similar case is seen in Persia, in the rising resentment against American aid in various forms which, in widespread popular opinion, has served no other purpose than to keep a corrupt political system and its privileged supporters in power. In both cases it was the psychological effects of technical and economic works that produced the most significant change—and the changes were not in our favor.

Our—or NATO's—vast military program in Turkey probably achieved its policy objective in strategic terms, and, at least for a time, in psychological terms as well. Both Americans and Turks wanted the same thing—up to a point—and the joint effort went well. But the economic consequences of the military works included disproportionate budget allocations for military purposes, infusion of inflationary funds, withdrawal of prime manpower from productive services, and diversion of attention from other needs. And these economic consequences may have had as much to do with the general collapse of Turkey in the late 1950's as anything done by the three ministers who were hanged for their part in the collapse.

My own knowledge of events in Persia leading up to the oil nationalization of 1951 and to the subsequent economic and political collapse of that country has convinced me that American political action alone could have brought about precisely the changes needed at that time to resolve the issues in which the Shah, the Persian people, and the British were then crucially enmeshed. Given our political support with its psychological side-effects, the Shah, according to his own assertion at the time and to other evidence, could and would have exercised his constitutional—if less than wholly democratic—powers to take control of his pusillanimous government, approve the pending oil agreement, and get on with his Seven-Year Plan. Here was a clear case of no policy objectives at all on our part, no sensing of the changes that were needed and wanted in Persia and that would have served our own national aims. After the collapse we ineptly chose economic instruments—always our favorite ones—though the first changes needed were manifestly political, social, and psychological. The side effects of our loan offers were what should have been expected—contemptuous rejection by the articulate public and heightened stature for Mossadegh for his refusal of those offers.

An interesting example of the secondary effect of a public health operation was seen in a malaria control program in Persia while the first Seven-Year Plan was still under way. Village spraying with DDT was in high demand by the villagers themselves—not to eliminate anopheles mosquitoes, which were not associated with malaria in the villagers' minds, but for prompt riddance of fleas and lice. The Minister of Health used the Near East Foundation for technical guidance, but had a policy objective of his own. Instead of confining the program to a single region of the country and spraying every village in it as had been done before, he took one village out of five or six, concentrating on areas in which discontent with the government had been most serious. This resulted in an immediate and widespread realization among the people that the Shah's Seven-Year Plan actually reached down to their level, with renewed expectations among the skipped villages that their turn would come soon.

Amusing but significant evidence of the impact of this program upon the people arose from the practice of the spraying teams to mark each hut or house with a number and the symbol "DDT" in red paint to show that it had been sprayed. These quickly began to be used as addresses. A certain family lived in "DDT number so-and-so."

Another illustration will show how the perceptive sel
tion of policy objectives with matching operational obje
tives brought about changes which had proved stubborn under earlier treatment. During the middle 1950's a broadly
conceived "objective"—whether policy or operational might
be questioned—was agreed upon between Turkish and American officials. The change envisaged was a vast increase in the
volume of wheat produced on peasant farms, to supplement
the output of state farms and produce a surplus for export—
badly needed for balance-of-payments reasons. The course
adopted to bring this about consisted mainly of an extensive
system of modern wheat silos and ship-loading facilities. The
construction program went on haltingly and expensively for
a year or two, but the farmers' production showed no increase despite those preparations for a market outlet. Wheat,
except on a few mechanized state farms, was traditionally a
subsistence crop and it remained so.

Then Harvey Bross appeared on the scene, an experienced
American agronomist—practical type—representing American aid. He persuaded his anxious Turkish colleagues that
the *first* policy objective in this situation was to make the
peasants *want* to produce more wheat. With this in mind
Bross stopped the work on the elaborate storage and shipping
facilities at the ports. Through *Toprak,* the government
grain-handling agency, a local wheat-buying agent was established within easy reach of every wheat-farming village. Cash
was advanced for buying seed, and paid on the spot for wheat
delivered, which was stored in straw-lined pits in the ground.
Additional acreage was promptly put under cultivation by
the peasants, who were willing enough to work but until then
had seen no reason for producing more than they could use.
The nearby straw-lined pit was the answer. It was their cash
market. Meanwhile arrangements were made for intermediate
collection stations where the wheat was piled in heaps above

the ground, and other facilities were provided as needed to move it to main distribution and shipping points. By the following season substantial quantities had been accumulated, and Turkey began to export wheat. Bross had no further difficulty in showing farmers how to increase and improve their crops.

What happened was that the initial policy objective, sound enough as a starting point, was broken down by Bross until each part could be identified not only with a particular change, but with an operational objective that brought this change about. The initial operational program—before Bross arrived—may have brought a new goal within sight of the wheat farmers, but not within their reach. What was missing was a realization on the part of those who devised it that people seldom leap gaps from old ways to new ones; old ways must be changed into new ways. This is what Harvey Bross knew—although I never heard him talk about policy or operational objectives.

Nasser, in Egypt, has exhibited a greater virtuosity in the use of one kind of instrument to produce another kind of effect than has any other Middle East leader in recent times. This warrants closer attention than it has received by our own policy-makers. Nasser's record, on the whole, supports the judgment that his actions are not haphazard; he seems to have known what he wanted and how to get it. Nevertheless, many things that he has done can be rationalized only on the assumption that what he really wanted was the indirect rather than the direct result of what he did.

A list of his conspicuous actions during the last few years would include his part in the following:

Organizing the coup of 1952.
Initial support of Naguib as national leader.
Expulsion of Naguib and succession as leader.

Rabble-rousing tactics against Israel, the British and French, and the foreign oil companies operating in the Middle East.

Breaking with the British over occupation of the Canal Zone.

Nationalization of the Canal, following the withdrawal of Western offers to finance the High Dam at Aswan.

Overtures toward the Soviet Union.

Efforts to create Pan-Arab and Afro-Arab unity.

The creation of the United Arab Republic.

Opposition to the Baghdad Pact and the Eisenhower Doctrine.

This list could be extended, still limiting it to actions taken by Nasser himself in the various situations that faced him, but these instances are enough to make my present point. All the operational objectives indicated by the foregoing actions, however diverse in kind, appear to have been directed toward the single policy objective of winning popular support as a leader. That is, Nasser was solving over and over again the same problem, as it appeared to him and in ways that were only circumstantially different, of gaining and preserving the authority that was necessary for achieving the national goals to which his cause was dedicated. Every one of the operations named was exploited to the full for its psychological effect in uniting his people behind him, as the leader on whom they could depend for security against external threats.

There was pressing need for such unification if his political system was to survive, for the greatest threats to it came from rivals within Egypt itself. Powerful groups with vested economic interests had suffered heavily as a result of his actions. Powerful political groups opposed his arrogation of authority. If he had permitted domestic affairs to become the critical issues, Nasser could scarcely have hoped to retain leadership over such opponents. But in the face of external threats—real or fabricated—rivals within the country were silenced by the people's acclamation of Nasser as their savior.

During this period of Nasser's operations, which lasted from 1952 to around 1958, he showed little evidence of concern with immediate social or economic reforms. Prosperous factories were closed down, or largely so, when he confiscated British and French shareholders' interests and put men of his own on the boards of directors, thus shutting off the companies' sources of raw materials and their markets—both mainly in Europe. And even though Egypt was at that time short of schools for approximately one-third of its school-age children—and most of the schools it had were staffed by untrained teachers—competent Egyptian teachers by the hundreds were sent to neighboring Arab countries where their most visible activity was spreading pro-Nasser propaganda. The Aswan High Dam project was made to order for his purposes; if he obtained the necessary financing he would be hailed for the accomplishment, even though the benefits were many years away. If the aid were refused it was further evidence of the enemy outside the door.

All of Nasser's actions could be rationalized on the basis of his attempts to win popular support. Perhaps if our own policy-makers had recognized this we would not have reacted to his apparent hostilities and inconsistencies with our own hostilities and inconsistencies which played into his hand. If it was political security that he needed and wanted as a prerequisite to getting on with a program of national development, our own policy-makers might have found ways to help him establish that security without the necessity, on his part, of creating dangerous situations and dangerously extricating himself from them as a means of winning support.

Since about 1958, Nasser's policy objectives seem to have turned increasingly toward the advancement of his people and toward providing the mechanisms of government that are necessary for achievement rather than for survival. It seems reasonable to suppose that the continued acceptability of his government by the people will depend largely upon his success in this field.

The frame of reference provided by the capabilities of various means to implement change brings attention to another consideration in fitting policy objectives and operational objectives together. This is the broad distinction that can be made between changes in conditions and changes in behavior.

The term conditions refers to the non-behavioral environment within which behavior takes place. Conditions include such things as climate, soil fertility, availability of water, systems of communication and transport, housing, natural resources, foreign-exchange balances, and the like. Since a policy objective is defined as a change in behavior, changes in conditions are excluded. The policy-maker is concerned with conditions only as they affect behavior. To know how they affect behavior is crucially important—a key part of our general problem. Most, although not all, operational objectives are aimed at changing conditions and thus indirectly bringing about changes in behavior. Exceptions are the operational objectives to be reached through direct influence upon behavior, for example, by educational or psychological programs.

From the policy-maker's point of view—if not from a strictly logical one—changes in conditions differ in two important respects from changes in behavior. The first distinction is that, whereas the behavior of a person or group is continuous, and change is manifested by a difference in that behavior at two points in time, this is not necessarily true of changes in conditions. That is, most conditions that are designated as operational objectives can be produced quite independently of pre-existing conditions. This gives the policy-maker a much freer hand in fixing criteria for the selection of operational than for policy objectives. Thus a new factory of any kind can be established at any place at any time—given the resources. So can a new agricultural credit bank. Some Middle East countries have been sprinkled with both. But in many cases their doors have soon closed because the behavior that also must be changed in order to operate and make use of those changes in conditions cannot be influenced in any other way than by starting with the behavior that already exists and changing it into the kind of behavior that is required. The rates at which successive changes take place may vary widely, but there is no discontinuity. It is a fallacy —not always avoided—to suppose that persons or groups can be disembodied in one context and recreated in some entirely new set of circumstances. Policy objectives must be arranged in such sequence that each new change begins where the preceding one left off.

The second distinction between conditions and behavior that is important to the policy-maker is that the means through which conditions can be changed is usually quite obvious; the capabilities of our ordinary means are well known. But the factors that determine behavior, which influences the success or failure of a change in conditions, are less well known. Thus the selection and priority of both policy and operational objectives, with any given national aim in view, rests fundamentally upon our understanding of what makes people do what they do, and what would cause them to do something else.

With the Eisenhower Doctrine serving as an excellent example, a large part—perhaps most—of what has passed for American "policy" in the Middle East has been intended to safeguard our national security. National security has—and deserves—highest priority among our American aims. In considering our Middle East policy we can leave aside the question of missile-launching bases, military airfields, and other direct extensions of our own defense system that merely hap-

pen to be located in the Middle East. Of course the utility of
even those facilities depends upon the relations that we have
established, through our policy, with the governments and
people concerned. But the American security interests that
most concern us here focus upon the threat of Communist expansion in the Middle East. As events of the last few years
have shown, there is a possibility that "limited wars" within
the area might grow to dangerous proportions because of
Communist involvement.

There are a number of ways in which existing situations
should be changed to give us the security we seek. What
policy objectives should be set to define those changes? To
answer this we must know how Communism seems most likely
to spread in the Middle East—not merely how it spread in
eastern Europe or in China. This requires a much closer
knowledge than we now have of Middle East society, for
Communism either spreads or is resisted in the minds of
people and in their social and political institutions.

The threat of direct military invasion of the Middle East
by Communist powers does not presently appear to be a serious one. To vanquish an invader is a policy objective, and
one operational objective clearly indicated—with such priority as competent military judgment gives it—would be to
strengthen military capacity to resist invasion. However, the
strategic or tactical value of any military force that could be
built in any Middle East country except Turkey is question-
able, and the other effects of such a course raise grave doubts
as to its wisdom. Even in Turkey, where a massive military
program could be most strongly supported by claims of
strategic value, the economic strains of the NATO military
program almost certainly accelerated the Turkish economic
collapse. In Persia and all the Arab countries it is an open
question on whose side the army would fight, either in a war
between the West and the Communist powers or in a limited

regional conflict. What may remain mere uncertainty on these points might be raised to actual danger by equipping them for modern warfare.

A threat to our security far more serious than that of military invasion by the Communists is that substantial numbers of the Middle East peoples, or those who exercise authority over them, will choose to align themselves with the Communist powers. Our policy objective here has high priority. It is *to move them to reject that choice*. This objective, it should be noted, is not defined as aligning the Middle East countries with the West—which is another matter entirely—but persuading them *not* to become aligned with the Communists. The distinction is important. The operational objectives that are indicated in the two cases are quite different. We would not, for example, repeat the abortive operational objectives represented by the Baghdad Pact, the Middle East Defense Pact, or the Eisenhower Doctrine, each of which backfired seriously in our disfavor.

Various possible reasons why Middle East peoples might choose to align themselves with the Communists can be recognized, and in each case some change in an existing situation can be defined as a policy objective. The first reason is clear, though our policy-makers have been remarkably slow in recognizing it. If the *only* choice open to the Middle East peoples or to their political leaders is to join either the West or the Communist camp, a long history of Western domination and exploitation loads the scales heavily against the West, and will continue to do so until widespread memories and prejudices have been erased by positive remedial action. Therefore the choice of non-alignment must be left open and given legitimate status. This can be done by making it clear that the United States asks no country to join it in its conflict with the Communist powers. It asks only that all countries accept and defend the right of self-determination as a basic social and political principle. This in itself is not "neutrality." It is the *right to choose neutrality*. It is also fundamentally opposed to the Communist doctrine, which recognizes no such right.

To inculcate this principle of self-determination requires that operational objectives be set for both our diplomatic and our mass-information agencies. Expertness is required, for these techniques are not for novices. But expertness alone is not enough; the wrong things must not be done even though they are done well. Guidance is required, and must rest upon a realistic understanding of the cultural and institutional developments that are necessary for the practical application of the principle of self-determination.

The exercise of social and political self-determination does not mean progressive fragmentation into units that are completely independent. Such an interpretation makes the principle meaningless. On the contrary, the principle is a unifying one. It tends to assimilate groups within which certain rights are recognized into larger groups that have the capability to preserve those rights. The communication of this idea to peoples of different cultures, languages, and special interests necessitates a knowledge of those peoples. Particularly in the case of mass propaganda, specific audiences must be identified in terms of the ideas they already hold, and their susceptibilities to change made the basis of the propaganda approach.

The inculcation of the principle of self-determination as a right of all people would be the most powerful resistance to Communism that could be engendered in Middle East minds. This is mainly because it is in basic conflict with Communist doctrine, but this is not the only reason. The principle is a fundamental one in unifying social groups of every kind from the family to the nation, including groups based upon such attributes as race, religion, or language. The right to maintain group freedom is strongly held in traditional societies, and this is noticeably so in the Middle East. But groups overlap, and a large one may include many small ones. Conflicts among group interests are inevitable. The vigor with which a group right will be defended depends upon the value placed upon that right. We can identify Middle East groups which are bound together by attributes that are inherently opposed to Communism. We should set as policy objectives, at least in certain cases, the strengthening of such groups.

The argument for this is more than the obvious one of reinforcing positive opposition to Communist ideology. Both reason and historical evidence show the strategic importance of stopping Communism at the threshold of any social unit that feels itself bound together by ties that are stronger than their ties with those outside. Once Communism has penetrated such a group, resistance to its spread inside is lowered by its acceptance by some members of the group. The question is raised in their minds: if it is good for some, why not for all—or at least preferable to group disunity? Many examples of this process in action can be seen outside the Middle East. One is the spread of Communism in southeast Asia. The difficulty—or impossibility through means at our disposal—of halting the Communist rebels in Laos arose largely because of the disinclination of the non-Communist national forces to fight against a rebellious movement that already had been accepted by a large segment of their own people. Acceptance of a Communist regime in the Indian province of Kerala is another case in point. Another example is the Castro revolt in Cuba. In the latter case an immediate effect was seen in the changed attitude of most other Latin American peoples when the fight against Communism meant fighting against a fellow member of the social system which identifies itself as being Latin American.

Within the Middle East the Communists have been adept

at recognizing social groups that can be turned against the West, and then exploiting the group affinity to facilitate the spread of Communist influence—the oppressed peasants of Azerbaijan, the Kurds who were denied nationality, political groups in revolt against "Western imperialism," economic groups with appetites for accelerated industrialization, and intellectual groups in revolt against social injustice. They also create new groups for the same purpose—political parties under various names, and youth groups under many disguises.

It is important that our Middle East policy give attention to this aspect of social behavior. The strategic principle involved—to state it in homely terms—is to keep the rotten apple out of the barrel rather than try to control the spread of the rot inside. The barrel, in this case, is any social system in which the unifying forces are stronger than the divisive force introduced by Communism as the people believe it to be. From this point of view the policy objective that must be sought and suitably defined in each case is the strengthening of whatever social-system attribute—or as many of them as possible—is recognized as being opposed to Communism. There are many such attributes. The urge for self-determination is a pervading one; it is at least latent in nearly all social groups and becomes dominant in nationalist movements— both state and Arab. Religion is another.

Islam has been a strong unifying influence among its followers, but the fact that many millions of Moslems have been living for years within the Soviet Union and Red China has made a breach in this barrier against Communism. The number of Moslems who have defected to Communism within the Middle East as a whole is still relatively small. But the rotten apple is in the barrel, and the conflict in basic precepts has never been made a crucial issue by the Moslems—and certainly not by the Communists. An operational objective here would be to reanimate as a militant force the belief that "there is One God and his name is Allah," and set this against Communist atheism. A corresponding objective might be set for Christian social systems within the Middle East.

Still other group attributes can be found and similarly employed for strengthening group resistance to Communist penetration. A broadened concept of popular representation in government might serve in some cases, that of free private enterprise in others. But to catch up with the Communists in the technique of using group solidarity as an instrument for the extension of influence, we Americans must know much more than we do now about the existing social structure of the Middle East, and what ideas and beliefs need to be implanted, strengthened, or combated in order to resist group penetration by the Communists.

I can describe from my own experience an almost incredible case of group solidarity doing the Communists' work for them—or almost doing it. That it should have happened in Turkey, the last place in the Middle East where it might be expected, is hard enough to believe. The fact that the group concerned was the most progressive segment of the society—the energetic private businessmen and factory-owners in the main centers of the country—makes it even more incredible. It was in 1955, when nearly all industrial activity was severely cramped by the shortage of foreign exchange for imported raw materials and spare parts, and production was substantially curtailed. Prime Minister Menderes was attending a conference in Karachi, and had just broadcast his refusal to consider a proposal by a Communist trade mission to enter into direct negotiations with Turkish private industrialists for the supply of their requirements on liberal terms of credit. Simultaneously with that offer and its proclaimed refusal in Karachi, the terms of the Communist offer were made known—no one seemed to know how—in each of the main industrial centers in Turkey.

During the remainder of that day and part of the following night I remained in close touch with the President of the Union of Chambers of Commerce and Industry in Ankara, and was permitted to review the swelling volume of demands from the various regional Chambers that private businessmen be permitted to avail themselves of the offer. This started with a few inquiries that were ignored by the central authorities, but quickly became a stampede that was stopped only by the return and decisive action of the Prime Minister. The Union of Chambers of Commerce and Industry is one of the most highly organized institutions in the country, and nearly all businessmen, in the modern sense, are members. In addition to this formal mechanism for the unification of action, the common interests and personal attributes of the private businessmen, identified them as a group. Once the stigma of dealing with the Communists had seemed to be removed by the action of a few members, the attitude of the entire group was affected.

It might be asked, where were our own economic aid experts while this was going on? I could be wrong, but my guess is that they were too occupied with reports on large projects, such as steel mills and dams, to concern themselves with what the Turkish businessmen wanted.

But the choice between accepting or rejecting alignment with the Communists is not made solely by the people, even in response to group consensus. As in all traditional societies, social groups generally in the Middle East depend heavily upon their leadership for decision-making. And leaders have reasons of their own for what they do.

There is not a Middle East country in which the government has not been overthrown or critically endangered at least once in the last ten years. Every new government has been faced with internal opposition that has threatened its survival. Rival leaders, in such circumstances, seek support wherever it can be found. American support, when given, usually goes in the conventional way to the government in power. Opposition leaders turn to the sources that are left, including all anti-government factions and the Communists. Mossadegh's coup against the Shah was organized in this way; so was Kassem's in Iraq. And when Western support is withheld from a government in power, the government itself turns elsewhere. We cannot counter this by labeling it "blackmail." It is part of the mechanism of political survival. Subordinate leaders use the same tactics, and most popular leaders carry their followers with them, whatever the basis of the group affinity.

To deal with this widely prevalent cause of alignment with Communist powers we must know more than we do about the part played by group leaders in Middle East society. What are their objectives, and what do they require to achieve them? How do they gain popular acceptance, and what determines their relative rank? All this and much more is involved in the process through which government is established in a Middle East country, or one government instead of another.

The belief seems to have been widely accepted in American minds—public and private—that poverty, oppression, and despair among the peoples of backward countries are the chief causes of their embracing Communism. This belief has led to the conclusion that "raising the standard of living" and "helping people help themselves" is our first line of defense against the spread of Communism in those countries. Quite apart from the fact that such clichés are useless as guides for policy and operational objectives, this belief itself has led us away from fruitful objectives as often as it has led us toward them.

Poverty, oppression, and despair are among the chief factors that commonly lead to popular rebellion against whatever government is in power. But in nearly all cases it is the leaders—not the suffering people—who make the choice for or against Communism. And it is by no means established that leaders who choose Communism do so to cure poverty, oppression, and despair among the people. On the basis of Middle East evidence, one must conclude that leaders are more ready to exploit popular distress as a means of increasing their own following than to cure the distress—an example is the attitude of most Arab leaders toward a million Palestine refugees. This has been so whether the leaders turned toward or away from Communism.

Popular distress breeds rebelliousness and internal conflict, and most conflicts give the Communists an opportunity to support one side against the other, and thus gain entrance into the affairs of a country. To avert conflicts that might have this result may in some cases be a policy objective of our own. But combating Communism is not our only reason for seeking ways in which we can bring about or accelerate social, political, and economic development. To begin with, we have accepted certain commitments, bilaterally or through the United Nations, which we must discharge. Also, Americans wish to live in a world that is as nearly free as possible from conflicts that might lead to war; and wide extremes of privilege and privation are not conducive to that kind of a world. Moreover, quite apart from our concern in the welfare of others for its own sake, we wish to keep our own economy strong enough to serve our growing needs, and we do not believe that this will be possible unless the world's supplier and consumer markets grow prosperous along with us. All these are part of our postulated national aims, and lie in back of those aid programs that are not aimed directly at our security. In addition, despite wide divergences and imperfections in our own performance, Americans place a high value on social justice—at least as a goal to be sought. In most

American minds the image of physical and cultural privation that is associated with "backward peoples" produces a genuine desire to apply our resources to their relief, whether for high moral or simple humanitarian reasons.

But to know how to promote social and economic advancement we must know what now prevents or obstructs it. Here is where the changes that we define as our policy objectives must take place. We must not look solely at our own case, and prescribe for others what we found good for ourselves. Early Americans jumped over Rostow's "first stage" by eliminating the "traditional society" they found here, and made short work of the "second stage" by importing the "preconditions" that were not already here in abundance. But the realities of the Middle East situation are quite different.

Persia is a good case to start with, because almost all the factors commonly regarded as favorable to accelerated growth seem to have been present during the thirty-five years that have passed since Reza Shah took over. Throughout this time, except for a short period following oil nationalization, there was ample money for substantial investment, public and private, including both foreign exchange and national currency. There was much more agricultural land than was being used, also timber and mineral resources. As for human resources, around twenty million people were reasonably well distributed in respect to economic resources. A relatively small upper class was well educated in their own or European universities. This group included lawyers, economists, and engineers and other technologists. As for political organization, throughout the period there has been a constitution modeled on Western patterns, with an elected Parliament (Majlis) and a Council of Ministers. Except for the period 1941–1946 while the country was occupied by Allied forces, and except for Mossadegh's three years in power, the Shah has had all but complete dictatorial powers—if he chose to exercise them—

backed by the army and police.

During this thirty-five years the two reigning Shahs have launched three large-scale national development programs: Reza Shah from 1930 to 1940, Mohammed Reza Pahlavi from 1946 to 1951 and again beginning in 1954. The third program is still in progress during the early 1960's. In addition to ample financing, each of these programs has had the support of substantial foreign aid of various kinds: engineers and other technologists, consulting specialists, competent contractors, participation of foreign private entrepreneurs, and access to world markets for both buying and selling. Notwithstanding all this, a broad assessment of this thirty-five years of effort indicates that around ninety percent of the population is little or no better off than at the beginning. What has obstructed advancement?

This question also has pertinence in Iraq, where a capable British-installed government, backed by the army and with vast oil resources as a source of capital for development, brought little or no change to ninety percent of the population during the thirty years before its overthrow by Kassem in 1959. And this despite very large expenditures for what was referred to as "national development."

Everywhere we look, the pertinence of the question holds. In Egypt, both under the monarchy that fell in 1952, and under about ten years of Nasser's rule since then, ninety percent of the population is still a fair estimate of those whose lives remained unchanged. Even in Turkey, which has shown more progress than any other Middle East country, most of the visible improvement in social and economic conditions was concentrated in two periods of around five years each— the last five years of Ataturk's rule (1935–1940) and the first five of the Menderes government (1950–1955).

It is quite possible—and even may sometimes be necessary—for a program of national development to be based on the principle that a period of austerity must be suffered in order to accumulate savings. In the West, and perhaps also in the Communist countries, such a principle is well established. But in none of the Middle East countries has the capital that has gone into development been formed from "austerity" savings. The large oil-producing countries have had more capital than they have known how to invest, and Turkey, under Menderes, raised its developmental capital largely by deficit financing and American grants. The failure to show social advancement or to make economic progress cannot be laid to austerity.

It seems clear that the main reason for the lack of progress in these countries has been that resources were allotted to the wrong purposes. Too much has gone into projects that for a variety of reasons have yielded low returns or none at all in either social or economic terms. Too little has gone into undertakings that either would have yielded social or economic returns promptly or would have laid the foundations for later returns. A very large number of the ostensible indications of advancement—including factories and other industrial installations, and public works and services—have lacked the social and economic foundations that would make them enduring. No adequate provisions were made to supply the trained personnel necessary for their operation and maintenance, or to create the purchasing power to absorb their production, or to develop the social, economic, and administrative institutions that were essential for the utilization of those works by the society. And meanwhile far too little or nothing was done to ameliorate the distressing conditions under which masses of people lived, far too little that would have at least given them hope for the future.

Why did this misdirection of resources take place? It could not have been because of the lack of sound technical advice, or of competent execution of the separate projects. These services were amply available. The crucial error was in the *decision* to do one thing instead of another.

Who made the decisions, and why were they made? Nearly all the decisions were made by the government concerned, because state funds were chiefly involved. In the case of private investments, choice was severely limited, since it had to be adapted to state policy. Why the decisions were made is less easy to say; the reasons depended upon the objectives of the decision-makers—and men's real purposes are not always what they are said to be. It is important that we Americans recognize this fact, even though we may not know what the real purposes are. We have been too prone to give support without knowing what is being supported—or to withhold it without realizing what it is being withheld *from.*

But is it enough to know the objectives of the current Middle East leaders? Must we not know too whether or to what extent those objectives are also the objectives of the people? But of what people? Even within a single country there is a wide diversity of groups ranging from tribal communities to educated business and professional men, each group with its own ideas as to what objectives are to be sought and in what order of priority. Experience tells us that unless the people of a country have at least small hope of getting the things they want, dissatisfaction will become desperation, and rebellion will follow. To evaluate correctly the pressure of popular desire for change, we must know how the groups which exert that pressure are formed, what their goals are, and what is required to achieve them. This takes us deep into the structure of the society, its traditions and value systems. It is not what *we* think they need, but what *they* think they need that matters first. Later we might change their thinking.

The leadership accepted by these various groups is related in some way to the respective group goals, their priority, and the expectation of achieving them by alternative routes. How do these groups combine, as they must to make their united influence stronger than that of the government itself? We know this happens, but what is the process through which rival leaders subsume their separate interests in the common one of creating a new hierarchy of leaders? In a particular case, what special attribute or presumed capability is most highly valued in a leader? It is by no means always his control over military fire-power, even in the case of a military officer. At the outbreak of the Turkish military coup of 1959 the "shot heard around the world" was the shot the Turkish soldiers refused to fire into a mob of their fellow-countrymen, in defiance of the Prime Minister's orders. In Persia, Mossadegh merely neutralized the Persian army by replacing the high command with men of his choice, so that it could not be used against him. Have we oversimplified the way in which authority is transferred from one group to another, by crediting it to "angry young colonels" heading military coups? In most of the Middle East's military coups the factor that appears to have given the army the capability that was needed to bring about a change in government was its *organization* —its discipline and centralized direction—rather than its weapons.

Generally speaking, no other organization capable of unified effort on a national scale exists in the Middle East. The people are not much given to organized effort. When a political mechanism has been equally well organized, as in Turkey's case until its subversion by the Menderes regime in the late fifties, or as in Mossadegh's case in the early fifties, political leadership was chosen over military as a means of implementing rebelliousness. And before Mossadegh, Shah Mohammed Reza Pahlavi—with neither military nor political organizations to depend upon—gained his popular support largely through the promise the Plan Organization gave of social and economic reforms.

The evidence is that, whatever the means used for bringing about a change of decision-makers at the national level, the action itself has rested upon a ground-swell of popular discontent, as a mandate that legitimized rebellion. This process concerns us closely, for it is the one that is operating in the Middle East today. We are watching it in Persia, Turkey, Iraq, Egypt, Jordan, and all the rest. We would do well to understand it better.

We must now face an aspect of policy-making that puts those charged with this responsibility to their most crucial test. This is the problem of dealing with conflicts among our own aims. Such conflicts are inescapable. When policy-makers deal with realities, aims based upon general principles will often necessitate compromise courses. Policy must provide criteria by which choice and priority among conflicting objectives will be decided in particular situations. Inconsistencies in our conduct which result from random decision-making can work great damage on the achievement of our aims. But to give one consideration reasoned priority over another in a given situation is not inconsistency—it is the only way to assure consistency.

To assert that the principle of self-determination gives no one the right to embrace Communism does not contravene the principle. This is not to say that a people do not have this right of choice—but if they choose Communism they renounce the principle of self-determination because the Communist doctrine denies it. The principle itself, however, confers the right to choose non-alignment. But in cases to which the principle does apply, whose "self-determination" takes precedence? When conflicting rights are asserted, our policy must indicate priority among the considerations involved, and this is not the same thing as abandoning the principle. It is the only way to decide, from our point of view, how the principle is to be applied.

The Kurds provide a case in point. Under the principle of self-determination as asserted by Woodrow Wilson at the close of World War I, the Kurdish people demanded their nationhood, which was denied on various grounds. In the hypothetical event that the same claim were put forward today, say to the United Nations, our policymakers would be faced with a set of dilemmas. First, under the same principle, the rights of others must be considered: the rights of existing nations that would be partitioned or otherwise affected by this course; and the rights of dissenting minorities—or perhaps even a dissenting majority—among the Kurds themselves. The vast Mosul-Kirkuk oil fields also involve other than Kurdish rights. But this is not all. The capability of the Kurds to form a viable nation is also to be considered—not as a qualification of the principle, but of its application to the Kurdish case until that capability is believed to exist. Our security interests are also involved; would such a nation be dominated by the Communists? More broadly, would this be a step toward reducing tensions that now threaten peace in the region, or create even more dangerous ones?

The hypothetical case of the Kurds can be matched in most of its particulars by many actual situations that confront us in the Middle East today. The fragmentation of the Arab world by the Allies after World War I faces our policymakers with even more perplexing dilemmas—involving Arab and state nationalisms, rebellions against established governments, vast foreign oil interests, and the many problems that have grown out of the creation of Israel. Most of the issues in which we are concerned are of such a nature that both parties to a dispute can claim shelter under one or more of our proclaimed American aims, either because of a commitment we have made in the past, or because of a principle that we have espoused. The most troublesome dilemmas arise when the realities of a situation seem to make it necessary that we set aside, or at least compromise, a basic principle of our own. But this can happen, and does happen, and is difficult to explain to the American people who are not closely acquainted with the realities.

A common case is one involving American support of a "dictator." Dictatorship is anathema to most Americans. But merely to condemn dictators is not to define a policy objective. To bring about a certain defined change in the way a particular government operates may be an important policy objective, but it is most unlikely that the replacement at one stroke of an authoritarian government with a "democratic" government could be defined as an attainable policy objective in any present Middle East country except Turkey. Various other policy objectives will have to be defined and achieved to produce a foundation upon which a democratic government can rest, and these transitional policy objectives are not likely to be achieved quickly. They are not likely to be achieved at all unless they are first defined.

Americans place a high value upon law and order, social justice, and cultural and economic advancement for all peoples. But to reach these goals does not necessarily require a democratic political system as a first step. On the contrary, experience has shown that all these desirable aspects of an advancing but still "backward" society *could* be developed quickly under a colonial administration or a dictatorship, *provided that such government made these its real aims.* Otherwise, progress toward these aims must await the slow growth of literacy, political consciousness and understanding, administrative institutions, and proficiencies of many kinds that make a people capable of guiding their own advancement and executing the works essential to it. These requirements are not automatically provided by simply giving people the right to mark a ballot. In our own American society

the power of popular vote as a means of achieving popular
aspirations grew out of a long sequence of antecedent circumstances—few of which exist among the Middle East peoples,
except within limited groups. Our policy-makers cannot
dodge these dilemmas. Compromising our aims does not mean
abandoning them; in many cases it is the only way to achieve
them. To repeat, policy is concerned with what is possible,
not what is merely desirable.

In my own work in the Middle East I have been confronted, on a limited scale, by such problems as have just
been described; and my purpose in defining problems in
terms of their significant factors was to get beneath the superficial evaluations that Americans are so likely to make. I have
sought to make these problems more meaningful by referring
to the social sciences as a source of solutions in generalized
terms and principles that would at least provide a logical form
to follow in the analysis of particular cases. For this, new concepts were needed for thinking about new things. Simple
models were used to disclose the main frameworks within
which crucial factors interacted—of a changing society as new
desires were created and new scales of value were accepted;
of political evolution as new systems for the exercise of authority developed; and of national growth as it had appeared
to take place in the Middle East. This is to name only a few
problems and factors, but enough to make plain that our own
pattern of decision-making about changes to be sought in
these countries must be much improved to take into account
the factors that are crucially important.

For various reasons, those who have executive decisions
to make will not be able to halt the continuous stream of
events while they reflect upon cause and effect, and acquaint
themselves with what has been learned about human behavior. But policy-makers must draw upon all existing sources
for guidance as to what factors should determine decisions,

and how those factors should be weighted. It is in this way that policy-makers can control decisions, not by trying to make all the decisions themselves—which is likely to be disastrous.

Generally speaking, our national aims are distant targets, and "achievement" consists of step-by-step progress in their direction through explicitly defined intermediate objectives. Typically, the changes that must be brought about to attain those objectives are related in such a way that certain of them must take place ahead of others, or concurrently with others. This gives priority high importance as a factor in decision-making. The recognition of "preconditions" or "critical requirements" has been receiving increasing attention by those concerned with developmental problems. The importance of *sequence* of changes has been made evident by the repeated failures of efforts which do last things first. The works of Rostow, Galbraith, and Mason, some of whose works were cited earlier, are examples of advanced thinking by American economists on these points.

But if we Americans are to take an effective part in accelerating the advancement of traditional societies, or—what is even more important to us—safeguarding our own advancement, there are "critical requirements" which *we* must meet too; and we cannot meet them merely by creating new administrative organizations with new names for old functions. This has been tried before.

The critical requirements for us, if we are to fulfill the role we appear to have accepted, parallel the last three in Galbraith's list for underdeveloped countries. They are as follows: (1) clear and purposeful objectives, both *policy* and *operational;* (2) competent administrative apparatus; and (3) capital and specialized techniques. Because we have almost completely lacked the first we have not known how to provide the second, and have lavishly wasted the third.

Clearly stated policy, as defined here, would provide references by which policy objectives and operational objectives could be selected and tested, thus meeting our own first critical requirement. But to say this is merely to restate the problem. Sound policy is not revealed to a person simply because he has been made responsible for it. Both to establish policy and to execute the decisions reached, competent administrative apparatus is required.

Here we are concerned only with those aspects of organization and procedure that are directly related to policy. It goes without saying that competence of personnel and good organizational structure are important factors. Any organization, particularly a government one in which political considerations are bound to play some part, will include men with a wide range of competence. It is also true that there is no single form of organization that can be said to be the only effective one. In general, however, the lower the level of personnel competence and the looser the organizational structure and procedure, the greater the need for guidance in decision-making. Experience suggests that this need rises to a maximum in a typical government bureaucracy.

A single example, among the many that might be given, will make this need clear. One of the most frequently heard criticisms of our American aid program is that Congress is reluctant to appropriate funds for a period longer than one year, and even within that period surrounds executives of the aid program with procedural restrictions that make the effective use of the funds almost impossible. Nevertheless, in my own opinion—which is based upon long observation of actual aid programs in the field as well as upon hundreds of pages of testimony supporting the demands for aid funds—it would have been a clear abdication of Congressional responsibility to the American people to extend such authorizations in either amount or time, until provision had been made for more effective administration of aid programs. Those responsible for authorizing funds have lacked a knowledge of the criteria by which actual expenditures will be determined, or even dependable reports of accomplishments resulting from funds already spent. Without such knowledge Congress resorted to restrictive safeguards which made accomplishment difficult.

The problem of allocating institutional resources among various means of achieving institutional aims is by no means a new one in our country. Private American corporations, for example, have developed ways in which this can be done, with satisfactory assurance on the part of the trustees of corporate funds that executive agencies, before making expenditures, will test every proposed undertaking in ways that have been agreed upon. General appropriations are approved on this basis. Assurance of proper decision-making is kept current by factual reports on what has been done, in terms of the aims that were to be served. Failures sometimes occur, but their causes are remedied either by changing the criteria of decisions or by changing the executive who is responsible.

Thus a board of directors, starting with a knowledge of the aims of the corporation, may allocate certain resources to the achievement of a designated aim. The board knows that the executive to whom this particular undertaking is assigned has specialists available to him who are competent in their several fields. The board knows too that each practicable way in which the designated aim might be achieved will be subjected to an established set of criteria and that decisions will be made accordingly. Organizational structure and procedural detail may vary widely, but in substance the process is the same. The questions asked and the criteria used for decisions may be roughly as follows:

1. Why should this project be done at all? What would be the consequences if it were not done?

2. Why should it be done in this way? What are the alternative ways and their relative merits?

3. Why should it be done now? What gives it priority?

4. Does all of it need to be done? For example, if two thirds of the benefits can be gained with one third of the expenditure, is the remaining expenditure still justified? At what point do the diminishing returns warrant limiting the project?

5. Will the project as proposed give the benefits claimed, or will additional projects be required for this?

6. Are the resources allocated (or requested) adequate to complete the project as proposed?

Ordinarily, policy will be established not only by requiring that such questions be asked, but also by indicating how decisions are to be influenced by the answers. Thus it may be stipulated that the suitability of a certain project be affirmed by a specialist in that field; or that certain statistical evidence be obtained as a basis for a given decision; or that a certain type of risk be avoided; or that a specified minimum result must be gained to justify an affirmative decision, and so on. An essential feature of this type of management is the requirement that a final report be made—perhaps intermediate reports also—stating factually what resources were used and with what results in terms of the initial intention.

Such criteria of decision can of course be modified or elaborated to suit the kind of operation involved, and also to suit the degree of latitude that is allowed various executives. In principle this system distributes decision-making authority and responsibility over those who are in the best position to make particular decisions, but maintains control over the way in which decisions will be made.

It is true that the circumstances under which our national aims relating to underdeveloped countries must be accomplished involve many obscure and sometimes rapidly changing factors. But this does not mean that criteria for decision-making are not needed or that they cannot be devised. On the contrary, it is precisely this fact that makes policy so necessary. Our Congress and our various executive agencies with responsibilities for foreign aid programs could devise such criteria in much less time than they now spend in futile disputes over specific projects that may or may not be suited to future conditions. Congress would have better control than it now has over both the expenditure of our resources and the accomplishment of national aims. Executive agencies would benefit equally through the greater freedom such policy would make possible in utilizing allotted resources.

Although the illustration just taken is concerned mainly with foreign aid of various kinds, policy is by no means limited to programs of economic and technical aid. What has been said applies over the whole range of our national aims as defined or postulated by the executive agencies of our government.

This brings us back full circle to the questions raised in the first chapter. Why have the things that we have done in the Middle East failed to meet our own expectations or those of the Middle East peoples? And what can we do now to meet them?

Answers to these questions require a deeper knowledge of the peoples of those countries than we have had, or than we have now. Policy is concerned with people and what they do, or what they are likely to do in given circumstances. About the facts of Middle East societies that are relevant to our policy problems we know almost nothing beyond our superficial impressions. We need to know how their various societies are structured, the nature of their institutions and their cultural ways, and how these and many other aspects of Middle East life are changing under the impact of contemporary influences, or how they might be changed. There have been few competent studies in this field. The literature is sparse and oriented mainly to academic viewpoints, which limits its usefulness to policy-makers. And even if it were more abundant and more readily available, our policy-makers have shown little interest in familiarizing themselves with the principles and techniques that would be necessary for its interpretation and use. Partly, at least, because of this sparsity of knowledge, we have been deficient in the most basic of our own "critical requirements"—clear and purposeful objectives.

Increasingly during the last few years our centers of advanced learning have been turning their attention to the part that scholars can take in analyzing the problems of development in the traditional societies. Increasingly, too, clear-thinking men in government have been turning to the scholars for special studies in this field. Both these are hopeful signs. But generalized theory cannot guide operational decisions—to attempt it would be a risky business. Neither the theorist nor the policy-maker can take the other's place, nor can either do the job alone. The precepts of theory must be related to the facts of the concrete case. At present this gap is a wide one.

In the field of nuclear weapons Americans have mobilized such a force of physical scientists as has never been brought together before. At the same time we have held, and still hold, that such weapons should never be used, that instead, people should learn to understand one another and resolve their problems together. But we have made lamentably little effort to understand people. The real danger is not what a nuclear bomb may do. It is what people may do with a nuclear bomb.

But nuclear warfare is not the only thing that can destroy **the civilization that Americans have helped to build. If most** of the people of the world reject the principles upon which our civilization is based, it will have little chance of surviving for the rest. To meet this danger we must now mobilize as strong a force of men trained in the social sciences as that already mobilized in the physical sciences. These men, and the policy-makers who work with them, should pay no more attention to scoffers than was paid to those who scoffed a generation ago at much of the theory upon which our technological advances rest. Every research scientist, chemist, or engineer who was engaged in industrial development prior to World War I can remember how "theory" was derided by "practical" men until they were silenced by what theory did.

We must begin to use what we know about people, and as quickly as possible learn more. We already have much theory to draw upon—but it remains our forgotten knowledge. It may be what will save our civilization.

Index

Books Prepared under the Auspices of the
Center for International Affairs, Harvard University

The Soviet Bloc, by Zbigniew K. Brzezinski. (Sponsored jointly with Russian Research Center.) Harvard University Press, 1960.

The Necessity for Choice, by Henry A. Kissinger. Harper & Brothers, 1961.

Strategy and Arms Control, by Thomas C. Schelling and Morton H. Halperin. Twentieth Century Fund, 1961.

Rift and Revolt in Hungary, by Ferenc A. Váli. Harvard University Press, 1961.

United States Manufacturing Investment in Brazil, by Lincoln Gordon and Engelbert L. Grommers. Harvard Business School, 1962.

The Economy of Cyprus, by A. J. Meyer, with Simos Vassiliou. (Sponsored jointly with Center for Middle Eastern Studies.) Harvard University Press, 1962.

Entrepreneurs of Lebanon, by Yusif A. Sayigh. (Sponsored jointly with Center for Middle Eastern Studies.) Harvard University Press, 1962.

Communist China 1955–1959: Policy Documents with Analysis, with a Foreword by Robert R. Bowie and John K.

Fairbank. (Sponsored jointly with East Asian Research Center.) Harvard University Press, 1962.

In Search of France, by Stanley Hoffmann, Charles P. Kindleberger, Laurence Wylie, Jesse R. Pitts, Jean-Baptiste Duroselle, and François Goguel. Harvard University Press, 1963.

Somali Nationalism, by Saadia Touval. Harvard University Press, 1963.

The Dilemma of Mexico's Development, by Raymond Vernon. Harvard University Press, 1963.

Limited War in the Nuclear Age, by Morton H. Halperin. John Wiley & Sons, 1963.

The Arms Debate, by Robert A. Levine. Harvard University Press, 1963.

People and Policy in the Middle East, by Max Weston Thornburg, with an Introduction by Edward S. Mason. W. W. Norton & Company, 1964.

Africans on the Land, by Montague Yudelman. Harvard University Press, in press.

Counterinsurgency Warfare, by David Galula. Frederick A. Praeger, in press.